Consensus Politics in Spain
Insider perspectives

Edited by
Monica Threlfall

intellect™
Bristol, UK
Portland OR, USA

First Published in Great Britain in Paperback in 2000 by
Intellect Books, PO Box 862, Bristol BS99 1DE, UK

First Published in USA in 2000 by
Intellect Books, ISBS, 5824 N.E. Hassalo St, Portland, Oregon 97213-3644, USA

DP
272
.C659
2000

Copy Editor: Peter Young
Production: Sally Ashworth
Consulting Editor: Robin Beecroft

A catalogue record for this book is available from the British Library

ISBN 1-84150-034-8

Printed and bound in Great Britain by Cromwell Press, Wiltshire

Contents

Editor's Acknowledgements

The idea for this book originated in a series of guest lectures given by the authors at the London School of Economics, which were organised jointly by the Cañada Blanch Centre for Contemporary Spanish Studies and the Instituto Cervantes, and chaired by Professor Paul Preston. The contributions presented here were developed around the theme of consensus politics to reflect the debate emerging after the celebration of the 20th anniversary of the Constitution in 1998 – a psychological milestone in Spanish politics.

Production of the book owes much to the financial help received for the translations of the articles from the Association for Contemporary Iberian Studies, through its Chair, Teresa Lawlor, past Chair, Robin Warner and Treasurer, Jackie Cannon, as well as the support of the International Journal of Iberian Studies and its editor, Hugh O'Donnell. Thanks are due to José Amodia for a revision of the edited typescript, to Kathryn Phillips-Miles for the first version of the translations and to Frances Angliss for help with manuscript typing. I am grateful for useful comments on two chapters made by Donald Share and to Peridis for allowing me unlimited use of his cartoons and caricatures.

The Transition That Never Happened

Martin Morales' unsympathetic view of Francoist political continuity, as it might have been. He uses a familiar image and unwritten words from bullfighting: General Franco the banderillero hands the cape and sword to the matador ('da la alternativa', gives his former minister, Manuel Fraga, his big chance). But they are incompetent amateurs practising on the usual head on a wheel, and are about to finish off the already wounded Spanish people.

Preface

Paul Preston

In the 1960s, the most important initiative in the cultural and academic relations between Spain and the United Kingdom was launched by a Valencian fruit importer in London. The creation by Vicente Cañada Blanch of the Anglo-Spanish Cultural Foundation has subsequently benefited large numbers of Spanish and British scholars at various levels. Thanks to the generosity of Vicente Cañada Blanch, thousands of Spanish schoolchildren have been educated at the secondary school in West London that bears his name. Many British and Spanish university students have benefited from the exchange scholarships which have fostered cultural and scientific exchanges between the two countries. Some of the most important historical, artistic and literary work on Spanish topics to be produced in Great Britain was initially made possible by Cañada Blanch scholarships.

Vicente Cañada Blanch was, by inclination, a conservative. When his Foundation was created, the Franco regime was still in the plenitude of its power. Nevertheless, the keynote of the Foundation's activities was always a complete open-mindedness on political issues. This was reflected in the diversity of research projects supported by the Foundation, many of which, in Francoist Spain, would have been regarded as subversive. When the dictator died, Don Vicente was in his seventy-fifth year. In the two decades following the death of the dictator, although apparently indestructible, Don Vicente was obliged to husband his energies. Increasingly, the work of the Foundation was carried forward by Miguel Dols. His tireless and imaginative work for the Foundation in London was matched in Spain by that of José María Coll Comín. They were united in the Foundation's spirit of open-minded commitment to fostering research of high quality in pursuit of better Anglo-Spanish cultural relations. In the 1990s, thanks to them, the role of the Foundation has grown considerably. In 1994, in collaboration with the London School of Economics, the Foundation established in London the Príncipe de Asturias Chair of Contemporary Spanish History and the Cañada Blanch Centre for Contemporary Spanish Studies.

The London Centre is merely one of the Foundation's several initiatives, among which can be counted the Cañada Blanch Centre for Advanced Spanish Studies in Manchester which is the focus for the work on medieval and Golden Age Spain of a consortium of universities in the North of England. It is the particular task of the Cañada Blanch Centre for Contemporary Spanish Studies to promote the understanding of twentieth-century Spain. This work is carried on through the publications of the doctoral and post-doctoral researchers at the Centre itself and through the many seminars and lectures held at the London School of Economics. While the seminars are the province of the researchers, the lecture cycles have been the forum in which Spanish politicians have been able to address wider audiences in the United Kingdom.

Throughout the winter of 1997–8, the Cañada Blanch Centre for Contemporary Spanish Studies organised a thematic lecture series in collaboration with the Instituto Cervantes of London. Under the overall title of 'The Spanish Transition and its Protagonists' (*La transición española a través de sus protagonistas*), a number of key figures gave their vision both of their own role and of the democratisation process as a whole. The greatest disappointment of the cycle was the fact that Adolfo Suárez, Spanish Prime Minister throughout the key months and years of the dismantling of the dictatorship, was unable to accept the invitation to speak. However, his absence was compensated by the remarkably frank speech by his *chef de cabinet* during the period in question, the diplomat Alberto Aza.

The cycle was fortunate too in being able to include Suárez's great opponent and, in some respects, collaborator in the democratic transition, the Communist leader, Santiago Carrillo. In many respects, a duel between the two was one of the central features of the period. After his appointment as Prime Minister on 5 July 1976, Adolfo Suárez cited the dead-weight of the entire Francoist establishment and the fire-power of the armed forces, the police and large numbers of militant Falangists as reasons for cautious, not to say hesitant, progress towards a limited democratisation. Against this, the mass demonstrations and strikes which shook Spain throughout the spring and summer of 1976 were cited by Santiago Carrillo from his clandestinity as reasons for haste and comprehensive change. The trial of strength between them was a crucial factor in ensuring that the first elections, on 15 June 1977, were truly democratic.

It will be recalled that Franco had devoted considerable efforts to maintaining the spirit of civil war in Spain. He had fostered the culture of victors and vanquished right up to his death. In his last public speech, on 1 October 1975, the thirty-ninth anniversary of his elevation to the Headship of State, he told a huge crowd at Madrid's Plaza de Oriente, that Spain faced 'a masonic left-wing conspiracy within the political class in indecent concubinage with Communist-terrorist subversion in society'. It is extraordinary that thirteen years earlier, in June 1962, in an early rehearsal for a democratic transition based on compromise and consensus, monarchists, Catholics and repentant Falangists from inside Spain met exiled Socialists and Basque and Catalan nationalists at the Fourth Congress of the European Movement in Munich. Their task had been, in the words of the Christian Democrat, Fernando Alvarez de Miranda: 'to break with the past and leap over the river of blood that separated them'. The duel between Suárez and Carrillo helped carry Spain over that river of blood.

Once elections had opened the door to the creation of a democratic polity, the next task was the construction of its legal basis. The complex process of drafting a constitution and seeing it through parliament was one of the key elements of the passage from dictatorship to democracy. It was explained with clarity and honesty during the lectures by two members of the seven-deputy drafting committee known as the *Ponencia*. The *Ponencia* consisted of three members of Suárez's *Unión del Centro*

Democrático, Gabriel Cisneros, Miguel Herrero y Rodríguez de Miñon and José Pedro Pérez Llorca; Gregorio Peces Barba of the PSOE; Miquel Roca of the *Convergencia i Unió*; Jordi Solé Tura of the *Partit Socialista Unificat de Catalunya* and Manuel Fraga of *Alianza Popular*. Peces-Barba and Roca spoke with striking candour about the compromises upon which Spain's constitutional consensus was built. The work of successive UCD governments in power was reflected in the speech by Juan Antonio García Díez, a social-democrat who served as Minister of Commerce, under both Suárez and his successor, Leopoldo Calvo Sotelo, from 1977–82. A lighter note was struck by the remarkable contribution of the celebrated cartoonist, 'Peridis' (José María Pérez González) in which he dissected the role of humour in the transition.

This volume is a good illustration of the thinking behind the initial lecture series. It provides a view of the transition to democracy and of current challenges to the political consensus which made democracy possible, seen through the eyes of some of its principal protagonists, a view made available in the English language for the first time.

Needless to say, the initial stages of the process from the death of Franco until the fall of Suárez provided the most dramatic moments of the transition. However, they constituted merely the opening phase of a long historical evolution. It has been argued that the real transition began only after the defeat of the attempted military coup of 23 February 1981. The consolidation of democracy, what some have called the 'normalisation' of Spanish politics, has been the object of a sequel to the original lecture series. Spread over a longer period, this examination of subsequent developments in Spanish democracy has had the benefit of contributions from, among others, the Catalan President, Jordi Pujol, the Socialist Prime Minister during the period 1982–96, Felipe González, the Minister of Defence who undertook the major reform of the Spanish armed forces, Narcís Serra, and the Governor of the Bank of Spain, Luis Ángel Rojo. Further lectures are planned. It is hoped that the ongoing cycle on the structural consolidation of democracy may, together with its predecessor, foment Anglo-Saxon interest in Spanish politics. It is certainly a project that pursues the same ideals that originally inspired Vicente Cañada Blanch.

1. Introduction:

The challenge of consensus politics in Spain

Monica Threlfall

The dates of 20–22 November 2000 will mark a quarter of a century after Generalísimo Francisco Franco's death and the first twenty-five years of Juan Carlos's reign – remarkable for a king once nicknamed 'The Brief'. Equally remarkable is the fact that, while it cannot be said that events in this period of Spanish politics unfolded according to plan – that would have left too little room for the famed Spanish spirit of improvisation – they did unfold along lines which are broadly satisfactory to most of the people, most of the protagonists and nearly all observers.

Satisfaction in politics – almost a contradiction in terms – is sufficiently rare for it to be almost absent from examination by outside observers. Exceptionally, the sociologist Mario Gaviria set out to write his book *The Seventh Power: Spain in the World* from an optimistic point of view, with the express intention of telling the world what a civilised polity Spain was. The satisfaction expressed by actors who are insiders and practitioners is more common. In Spain it is derived in part from their natural interest in highlighting the successful aspects of the events in which they participated. But it also arises from a phenomenon which made it possible for the actors to build rather than destroy, agree rather than argue, and pull together instead of apart. This is the phenomenon of *el consenso*, consensus politics, widely identified yet infrequently defined or explained.

It is all the more appropriate therefore that this book should consist of a set of insiders' accounts both of the Spanish transition to democracy and of the tensions that currently beset that historic consensus settlement. We present the memoirs and reflections of well-known protagonists and witnesses to those unique events, two of whom were even authors of the ground-breaking 1978 Constitution itself. They are Alberto Aza, Adolfo Suárez's *chef de cabinet* while he was Prime Minister; Santiago Carrillo, leader of the influential Communist Party at the time; Gregorio Peces-Barba, co-author of the constitution and former President of the Congress of Deputies; Miguel Roca, co-author of the constitution, former second-in-command to the Catalan leader, Jordi Pujol, and head of its Parliamentary group; Juan Antonio Díaz López, former

1

cabinet minister and one of the architects of the UCD's economic strategy; and last but not least, the cartoonist Peridis whose daily pictorial interpretations of those events guided Spanish readers through the roller-coaster of surprises, thrilling surges of progress, nerve-racking setbacks, violent jolts and becalmed moments of those extraordinary few years. On first impression, readers would be forgiven for thinking that this book's main concern is purely with recounting the transition to democracy in Spain. It is not the case. Far from simply a nostalgic reflection on those times, its guiding themes are building the new consensus in Spanish politics throughout the democratic period, and in particular, sustaining it into the nineties; and its unifying thread is the nature of consensus politics and the challenges it faces at the turn of the century.

A characteristic of the abundant literature on transitions and the Spanish case, especially that written from a political science perspective, is the way it has encompassed explanatory models of system change, the dynamics and even the mechanics of the transition, the alignments of the different actors, political culture, and the influences on the process, whether external or domestic, socio-economic or institutional (Share, 1989; Huntington, 1992; Linz & Stepan, 1996; Higley & Gunther, 1995; Maravall, 1981; Preston, 1986 amongst many others). Yet the question of consensus has not been a prominent theme of the literature: consensus-building and maintenance has been at best an implicit theme of these concerns. As an explanation, one could say that to some extent, consensus was a heavily used word among the political leaders, media and practitioners during the actual unfolding of the transition, and thereby acquired many common sense meanings in widespread usage (del Aguila & Montoro, 1984). Nonetheless, it is an under-analysed concept in politics, featuring hardly at all in the work of such prominent contemporary democratic theorists as David Held, for example. This volume contributes to bringing it to the fore as a meaningful concept for the understanding not just of post-authoritarian politics, but of post-conflict politics in general.

There is no question that a long line of thinkers from de Tocqueville to Lipset and to Huntington have offered a number of explanations for what makes a democracy possible and what makes it thrive. For the former, democracy involved a balance between the forces of conflict and those of consensus. De Tocqueville's analysis implies that the two may exist simultaneously, with consensus there to mitigate conflict, as if it were a case of avoiding excesses. The possibility of consensus already exists and can be nurtured as a force for good.

The early American sociologist Lewis Coser's work is a classic reference in the debate about conflict and consensus in democracies, though it is not specifically about consensus[1], being about conflict, control and even the notion of unity. But he usefully reminds us that the distinction has long been made in political science from Aristotle onwards between conflicts over the basis of consensus and those taking place within the basic consensus (Coser, 1956: 75). The Spanish case was clearly one of the former, yet much of the writing is on the latter. Nevertheless, in his work there are frequent shifts between these two platforms for the breakdown of consensus. Consensus as an ideal type exists when a large proportion of the members of the society, particularly its decision-makers, are in agreement as to what issues have to be addressed and what decisions are required. It is the antithesis of coercion. It is also to be distinguished from acquiescence or conformity to any rules of the game which have been 'imposed by powerful superiors on powerless subordinates'. But rather than a static state of affairs, it is also the active process through which agreement between participant actors is brought about. Here we can hear echoes of the forging of the Spanish consensus. Nevertheless, for Coser, the active process (that which is forged by participants) brings a consensus that is also inherently unstable and dialectical. This is the case in so far as, in modern competitive politics, parties are involved in transforming consensus into dissensus and in reconstituting new states of consensus. As beliefs and standards in society change, yesterday's utopia becomes today's accepted wisdom (Coser, 1956). This is a dynamic view of conflict within the parameters of a basic consensus, rather than of the creation of the basic consensus in the first place. Is the Basque nationalist challenge to the Spanish political consensus one of the former or the latter? – an important question for understanding whether it is a menacing, destabilising phenomenon or one that can ultimately be integrated.

Lipset noted in the 1960s that we knew much more about conflict than about consensus because conflict and dissent had been studied more extensively, while the issue of integration and cohesion in stable democracies, and the study of factors that curtail extremism, had been virtually neglected (Lipset, 1963). He saw it as important to locate the sources of resistance to extremism in a polity, in other words, to understand how the consensus is maintained under challenge. He also held that too much consensus led to 'the end of ideology', the expression he borrowed from Shils (coined in 1955), and worse, it made politics boring – as the Swedes had already told him (Lipset, 1963: 440–1). At the time he did not think to ask the Spaniards, starved as they were of most of the politics and all of the consensus – while being satiated with the boredom – during Franco's first Twenty Five Years of Peace (*los veinticinco años de paz*), officially celebrated not long after, in 1964.

We are familiar with the notion that consensus is necessary to democracy. For Rustow it is even the basis for a democracy, and he gives Ernest Barker's 1942 definition for it: 'the Agreement to Differ' (Rustow, 1970: 337) though later in his famous essay he also finds it a nebulous and ambiguous term akin to compromise (p. 357). Rustow nevertheless believes a *prior* consensus is not a precondition for democracy, because this would be implausible: 'people who were not in conflict about some rather fundamental matters would have little need to devise democracy's elaborate rules for conflict resolution' (p. 362), therefore he situates consensus not amongst the preconditions but as an element in the process of transition to democracy. He follows Crick (1964: 24, cited in Rustow, 1970, p. 363) on this, in that Crick wrote that consensus was like a shared idea of a 'common good' which was of itself the process of practical reconciliation, not something prior to or above politics. This provides a basis for analysing the Spanish case, even though Rustow stops short of considering how, if it is not already present, consensus may nevertheless be conjured up – as it was in Spain.

Consensus as an active process in politics has not commanded a great deal of respect from more recent analysts. It is hardly discussed in comparative politics or political development. In the few references it merits, it appears as a rather passive state of affairs which politics can fall into, depart from or return to after conflict activity. For Middlemas for instance, consensus features in terms of its breakdown – conflict takes centre-stage – and the attempt to restore consensus is primarily an effort to banish conflict. Consensus-*building* as an activity appears to be of little interest to most analysts, and is absent from what is termed the 'defining characteristics of great political reform' (Oskenberg & Dickson, 1991). Yet in the Spanish case it would surely figure precisely as a defining characteristic of the transition.

Seen in terms of a politics of compromise, consensus is often associated with the Swiss system of government which leads to permanent coalitions of parties in which issues are fought out and compromised in cabinet, at the summit of politics, rather than in parliament. So for those who believe in the inevitability of a simultaneous presence of dissent in society, consensus politics is a practice which tends to ignore dissent in favour of focusing only on the area of common ground. In this view, consensus tends to ignore or override a sector of popular opinion, hushing up their voices, veering on the elitist.

When looked at as a question of governance, consensus, rather than a fundamental style, is associated with specific policy areas. The post-war consensus in British politics centred around policies of the welfare state and the state's ownership of key sectors of the economy, but ignored dissensus issues such as immigration, law and order and questions of morality (Middlemas, 1979). The term 'Butskellism' suggested somewhat disdainfully there were no policy differences between the Conservative and Labour Chancellors of the Exchequer, R.A.B. Butler and Hugh Gaitskell (Reilly, 1988: 167). Some areas of policy are particularly prone to consensus, namely foreign policy, as was the case in Europe in the post-war period (Sassoon, 1996).

The notion of consensus which students of the more traditional political science courses are likely come across is probably from Lijphart (1984). He divides democracies according to whether they practise majoritarian or consensus government, focusing on Belgium and Switzerland as his model, because they display restraining elements which prevent full majoritarian government. But on closer examination, consensus governments are, for him, those where power is diffused through processes of sharing, dispersal, distribution and delegation in order to restrict executive dominance (Lijphart, 1984: 30). In short, he does not provide a model into which Spanish democracy fits either by design or default, if Heywood's (1995, 1991) emphasis on Spanish executive dominance is correct.

The literature on democratisation, particularly that referring to the transitions from authoritarian rule since the 1970s in Southern Europe, Latin America and Eastern Europe, has somewhat revived the term. Here consensus is seen as the consequence of a degree of political restraint shown by the winners in new or born-again democracies. These are more likely to consolidate and prosper if a new government attempts to maintain a modicum of consensus by not pursuing highly contentious policies too far or too fast, especially where these policies seriously threaten other major interests (Potter et al, 1997: 528). In fact such limits on policy change are often established before the democratic transition is complete, in the course of preliminary negotiations (Huntington, 1992: 609–15).

Already from this brief review, themes emerge: consensus as containing an unstable equilibrium; as containing the seeds of dissensus – its own destruction; as a form of mutual restraint or self-limitation; and as the quasi-spontaneous lack of dissent, with its threat of apathy. So the concept does not appear to fit the Spanish case convincingly. To understand the Spanish case, consensus should, arguably, not be taken as a synonym for moderation or the simple abandonment of radical policies. Arriving at a consensus was a much harder nut to crack in the transition, for as Peces-Barba says, in the end all sides had to accept agreements that were '*not totally satisfactory for anyone, yet satisfactory enough for all*' (my italics, this volume). In Spain, it was the outcome of struggle, whereas, in other cases, such as the post-war consensus in Britain, it was more of a fortuitous occurrence, one could argue.

Among Spanish political scientists one finds consensus dealt with in the context of regime change. Del Aguila and Montoro (1984: 126–157) devote a chapter of their analysis of the political discourse of the transition to consensual arguments, finding consensus to be linked to reconciliation, and used as an argument to strengthen freedoms, and avoid confrontation. In a second set of meanings, they see it associated with moderation, tolerance and coexistence, and in a third, as referring to a national agreement and political pact. The third is the most relevant since it fits major events such as the Moncloa Pacts and the adoption of the new constitution – discussed in this volume – rather than to speeches and writings. They make the interesting observation that consensus was not always referred to favourably, and was also used, not quite as a term of abuse, but in a distorted way to signify elite pacts reached behind closed doors, excluding the people, typical of traditional Spanish oligarchies. (pp. 164–5).

In other works such as Cotarelo's, consensus is part of the movement towards regime change. In a six-stage model of transition to democracy, consensus covers the second half, stages four to six (1992: 13) In Cotarelo's view, the first consensus is termed 'the agreement about the past', meaning whether to bury it or not, whether to have a national reconciliation process or instead bring perpetrators of violence to justice. In other words, this stage of his model does not apply to Spain, given the noteworthy way in which Spain drew a veil over the issue of justice and reconciliation – none of the authors in this volume give it any specific mention. Cotarelo's second consensus involves the establishment of provisional norms to debate the definitive ones. It involves (following Rustow) an awareness of 'national community' and the need for participation. From this flows the avoidance of exclusions that may have disfunctional effects and even anti-system effects (Cotarelo, 1992: 14). Here Spain is a case in point, and the self-exclusion of the Basque Nationalist Party (PNV) from the Constitutional consensus is touched upon by Peces-Barba and Roca in this volume.

The third consensus is the definitive setting of the rules of the game, which is normally a compromise formula. It is essential that the formula should not be exclusively imposed by one party or group (Cotarelo, 1992: 14) without this suggesting that the system should therefore become consociational (as in the Swiss example in Lijphart's scheme) instead of majoritarian. This six-stage model is likened to del Aguila and Montoro's early (1984) analysis of the political discourse of the transition, where consensus is associated with reconciliation, moderation and pacts.

If consensus is to be analysed as a practice, Coser provides a useful starting point when he suggested (without the Spanish case in mind, of course) that consensus is brought about when 'recalcitrant actors are motivated (...) to forego egocentric patterns of behaviour through being welded together by a collective "we" ' (Coser, 1994: 108). Notions of the 'common purpose' and of a political community are also central to Huntington's analysis (1992). This strikes a chord for the Spanish case: what happened was not the spontaneous consensus of apathetic democracies, but the politically invaluable phenomenon of the emergence of a kind of third agent, the collective 'we'. Well over a decade later, Felipe González used the phrase when referring to how, during the transition, political actors had decided their own destiny which, he said, 'had as its core element the recognition of '*un nosotros* beyond the differences between parties' (González, 1999: 20). Through his use of we (*nosotros*) as a noun, he indicates the presence of another force, more active than an abstract 'shared destiny' or the spatial metaphor of 'common ground': a collective will or joint protagonism. The collective 'we' is clearly present in these accounts, though not always so explicitly. It is sufficiently strong for both Peces-Barba and Roca to defend its pre-eminence in the face of nationalists claiming to be excluded from it.

To understand consensus as a notion is also important because in the Spanish transition there were no third, or external, parties acting as arbitrators – only antagonists left to their own devices. For although in retrospect the King may be considered to have been neutral in terms of taking sides, or on the side of democracy, he was not the arbitrator at the time[2]. In the dispute between The Powers-That-Be vs. The People, both sides had to do their own adjudicating. There was no judge present to remonstrate against any unreasonable behaviour, or to rap any deviants over the knuckles. Of course, democracy was a guiding light that all were following, but there are many stars in the democratic firmament. In such a context, the collective 'we', if successfully invoked, becomes an alternative to the arbitrator and urges the antagonists to take responsibility for resolving their differences and for moving ahead.

A further distinguishing characteristic of the Spanish consensus is the way it played a role in a polity which had no history of it, no inherited precedents to return to, and little familiarity with its European post-war connotations. Spanish consensus was not engendered in a stable, let alone a well-integrated, society. On the contrary, it came into being in a context of social division and acknowledged political conflict. Here, consensus was a forged settlement in a context devoid of unprompted accommodation; it remains, as the accounts in this collection show, a political defence-mechanism against the resurgence of conflict. Perhaps precisely because it represents such a historical achievement, the flag of consensus is waved with pride, and sometimes brandished as a weapon to ward off perceived threats.

Del Aguila (1992) offers an analysis which offers insights into the sources that produced consensus. In his view consensus emerges out of the need for legitimacy of both the reformist and the *rupturista*[3] actors, which could only be gained if they convinced the public that they would be able to avoid frontal conflict. Fear of conflicts, of loss of order and security, and in the last instance, of civil war constantly fuelled the search for accommodation between adversaries keen to avoid converting each other into enemies. Consensus was the outcome from actions played out in successive 'playing fields' (del Aguila, 1992: 59–71). Both Aza and Roca refer to this underlying fear in their articles in this volume.

Neither is the Spanish consensus the resigned agreement of tired elites at the end of a long drawn-out battle in which the opponents have become hazy about what divides them. For Franco's death and the political uncertainties that followed exacerbated the possibility of renewed conflict. So the forging of consensus began in a boundary-less terrain in which a bounded space had to be staked out by the main actors, and within which they gradually acceded to conduct their business. Far from simple agreement, consensus began embryonically in 1976 as the space between disagreement, the shared margins of opposing views. In this way consensus was born, as Share (1986) posited, out of the *transactions* between opponents who make a series of deals while remaining adversaries, as between buyers and sellers who stay formally on opposing sides even after the deal is made. Spanish opponents remained locked into competition, still winning and losing during the sets of transactions, at the very least until these were carved into the stone of the Constitutional text approved by referendum in December 1978.

The grand transaction of the transition – *the ruptura pactada*[+] – had to be hammered out in a series of negotiations, a long drawn out process that only really started after Suárez was appointed and continued for two more years at least till the end of 1978. It was a process of hard bargaining, bluff-calling, hinting at compromises only to withdraw them, giving and grabbing concessions of varied orders of magnitude. It is worth remembering that the Law of Political Reform passed by the Francoist legislative assembly in November 1976 was *not* pacted with the opposition, who urged their supporters to abstain in the ensuing referendum (del Aguila, 1992: 62). Since the late 1990s, British readers will have become acquainted with the two-steps-forward, one-step-back rhythm of such transactions through the case of Northern Ireland, with its complexities, elaborate rituals and slow tempo.

It has been suggested that on the death of Franco there was a general realisation among the political elite and the public that the time for authoritarianism had long gone and that both left and right wanted to move to a democracy. Yet democracy *tout court* was never the main issue at stake. *Reforma o ruptura* as the public debate was termed, was about *how* and *how far* to move away from dictatorship. More particularly, while some essential pillars for democracy could be erected, it was not mainly these which were the subject of dissent in Spain. Previous attempts at living inside the democratic architecture had unearthed structural faults over regional government (Spain's 'stateness problem' to use Linz & Stepan's term), church-state and church-society relations, and land ownership and the primacy of private property, amongst others. In the 1930s, both sides had failed to live up to the demands and duties of democracy or to play by the rules (Preston, 1978). In the post-Franco transition, by contrast, they were forced to design all the features of the new building together. Suárez and the King had presented the initial plans, but the Law of Political Reform merely created more work. The events of that winter/spring 1976–7 could hardly have been foreseen and Suárez's sleight of hand when finding himself in an impasse – suddenly legalising the Communist Party on Easter Saturday when all were on holiday (causing one radio newsreader to stumble, gasp, and go off-air) – showed just how much the genius for improvisation (which Spaniards boast of) had come to his rescue. As Carrillo recounts, it was the uncharted, eleventh-hour responses which actually enabled the first election to be conducted under internationally acceptable conditions. Even more so, the outcome of that election, with its radically altered balance of forces, was evidently not part of any plan, not even of any contingency plan. The new-found strength which the voters gave to opposition actors, particularly the PSOE, and the way they weakened the post-Francoist conservatives, altered the terms of the negotiations during the constitutional debates, re-balancing left and right in a way that allowed the emergence of an awareness of a 'national community', inclusive of the formerly divided 'two Spains'.

This becomes very evident when the detail of the Constitution is examined. The text is little known to English-language readers[5] apart from the nine articles of the Preliminary Title and a few oft-quoted clauses on equality, the right to life and the autonomies, yet it has been called 'revolutionary' (eg. Gómez Puentes, 1995: 79). As Peces-Barba shows, an examination of the detail of the text reveals strong progressive sections, not just on citizens' rights and duties but in the way the widest range of freedoms are allowed without any attempt at curtailment or circumvention through the typical subterfuge of conditioning sub-clauses (of the type that begin with *siempre que* ... , or *mientras no...*) or even of contradictory articles. It is also particularly progressive on the role of the state as protector and guarantor of a socially balanced and economically equitable society (perhaps one should just say particularly 'seventies').

In addition to these, Title VII, 'On the Economy and the Treasury', emphasises the role of the authorities and the public sector. It starts off by subordinating the country's whole wealth to the general interest, whatever its form and whatever titles to it there may be, in other words it denies the inviolability of private property without any reference to due compensation. It goes on to recognise public initiative in economic activity: essential resources and services may be reserved by law for the public sector, especially in the case of monopolies. The 'intervention' of companies may be allowed by law if the general interest so demands it. It was precisely a similarly worded clause which allowed Salvador Allende's government in Chile to take into public management a large number of private firms and became the subject of violent controversy. Because of it, Chilean business sectors felt justified in calling for the overthrow of the government. The Spanish Title VII is all the more noteworthy since the Constitution started to be negotiated barely four years after Pinochet, a self-professed admirer of Franco, had launched his bloody coup (September 1973–August 1977). Other clauses in Title VII commit the public authorities to support worker participation in companies and cooperatives and, most notably, 'to establish the means which may *facilitate the access of workers to the property of the means of production*' (my italics). In Article 131 the State can, via a law, plan the economy in order to care for collective needs and to stimulate income and wealth *and its more just distribution* (my italics). The concepts and language are undeniably progressive and 'old' Left, a clear indication of how much the old regime was forced to give away before the settlement.

This is not to say that the Spanish State has fulfilled its mandate in this respect – that is another debate outside the scope of this book. Nor should one deny that on close reading much of this text is subject to quite harmless interpretations (e.g. even free market States reserve the right of compulsory purchase of property). But the key point to note is the extent to which the Spanish Right lost the battle over the Constitution's language and philosophy. In all its major functions, both mechanistic and normative, its guarantees of freedoms and rights, its policy-prescriptive function in economic and social policy, its understanding of the role of the State and of a *public ethics,* as Gregorio Peces-Barba puts it, the framework negotiated by the representatives of the two antagonistic sides, both still clearly linked in 1977–8 to the winners and losers of the civil war, owed much to the social democratic perspective of the era. This has become particularly notable in retrospect, in view of the rightward shift of both Right and Left in European politics, and goes some way towards explaining the affection in which the Constitution is held by most of the authors in this volume, most emphatically so by Peces-Barba, the PSOE's representative on the drafting committee.

Insider perspectives

Uniquely among books on Spanish history and politics, this collection contains a wholly original contribution from the transition's leading cartoonist, Peridis. For the first time he resorts to pen and paper to develop a written analysis of the sources that inspired the peculiarly Spanish brand of visual humour. He traces the influences on the new post-war generation of political cartoonists, who were attempting to comment on the conditions under a dictatorship, first and foremost to Goya – not for his humour of course – but for his outstanding eye for physical frailty and human cruelty. Peridis shows how cartoonists in the Franco era found subterfuges to communicate with their readers, often relying on their intelligent complicity to avoid the censors through understatement. Direct depiction of Franco and his cronies were mostly avoided. Instead, it was the petty bureaucrat, his evident mediocrity in no way restraining his self-importance, whom they were forced to make fun of.

It would have been fascinating to have been able to include in this volume a study of Peridis' own work, interpreting his political vision through his daily cartoon in *El País*, had this book not been authored by the protagonists themselves. Readers may nonetheless be motivated to form their own view and even advance some initial hypotheses on the basis of the small selection of his work we have been able to reproduce here. I will start with what will hopefully lead to a genuine new look at an unexplored angle in the study of the transition by suggesting that what is striking in Peridis's work is its paradoxical departure from Spanish tradition – the very tradition he associates himself with. Instead of black humour, emotional excess, cruel caricature, Peridis's gaze is above all an affectionate one, poking fun at all the protagonists of political life, without robbing them of their self-image or seeking to destroy relationships of trust between them. Perhaps, like the authors of this book, he was keenly aware of the fragility of the process (like Suárez with his crystal cup in Aza's account) and wanted to find a way of capturing and commenting on his subjects in a manner that might leave them exposed, but never humiliated. In this way, through images which are revealing yet ultimately respectful, Peridis too served and preserved the Spanish consensus about the limits of the allowable during a particularly successful time in Spanish history.

We are also able to present readers with the first insider account in English of Adolfo Suárez's premiership, given by his former *chef de cabinet*, the career diplomat Alberto Aza. He underlines the vigour with which Suárez pursued democratisation once he saw that his great political opportunity lay with democracy. The birth of consensus stemmed from what Aza terms Suárez's *voluntad de diálogo*. He brought political actors into the warm hearth of elite bargaining from the cold of opposition or grassroots activism, and also pursued reciprocity in the talks. The account shows Suárez as the consummate political improviser making the most of every occasion that presented itself, in the midst of an unpropitious political climate, and with scant resources at his command.

Much has been made of the transition being founded on the legality of the Franco institutions, but lest this give the impression that these were solid, well-endowed bodies, Aza reveals the unexpected weakness of the Spanish state, despite decades of centralising bureaucratic control. Here the transition is in fact represented as a fragile crystal cup often on the point of being shattered. Those who are most often playing carelessly with it are not so much the traditional forces of conservatism – the armed forces or the church – as the band of politicians around Suárez in the UCD.

It was the UCD who tripped Suárez up. Aza insists that it was not threats from the military that caused him to resign suddenly, but internal disputes. In retrospect, resigning was probably the worst decision of his life, since he was never to make the comeback he evidently hoped for. It was also the decision that was indirectly, in the long run, to lead to one of the distinguishing features of the party system: the absence of a Spanish centre party. The electoral system's mechanism penalises nationwide small parties while encouraging a variety of regionally-based ones, but it is an irony that the very period of history whose characteristic political style was consensus and the search for the middle ground should simultaneously see the demise of more than one political option (the Christian democratic groups, the UCD and CDS) which sought to represent this middle ground electorally. This a phenomenon Aza clearly regrets.

The former Minister, Juan Antonio García Díez gives one of the most detailed and accessible accounts available to date to show how the UCD struggled under the legacy of over three years of unbalanced, even incoherent, responses to the first oil price shock. At the same time, he makes a consistent case for the coherence of the policy response of the UCD, later much-maligned in the conventional accounts of the period. He emphasises the way the UCD understood that the socio-political context would unavoidably mould their economic policy choices. New economic actors were rather suddenly able to have a far greater say in public life, altering the previous policy environment with a sudden tug. In particular, the new situation released demands that had previously had no outlet for expression: on the part of society as a whole, demanding more public services; on the part of trade unions, for higher wages; and on the part of the newly autonomous Communities, for more resources.

Within such constraints the UCD opted in the main for an incomes policy and increased public spending, and instituted a major tax reform to counteract its effects. While claiming that the UCD saw the need for a shift in the State's role, from omnipresent regulator to provider of public services, he nevertheless criticises as a lost opportunity its failure to ease the regulatory labour relations framework enshrined in the Workers Statute. In the UCD's defence one might interject that the increased strength of the trade unions, recently benefiting from the 1979 company-level elections of workers' representatives (*elecciones sindicales*), did not provide the appropriate climate for a reform that they would have tenaciously resisted, no doubt backed by the PSOE. On the latter, he provides a frank critique of PSOE's behaviour in opposition with regard to economic policy.

Santiago Carrillo, perhaps more than any other contributor, is the politician who faces the challenge of giving an account of events while avoiding the temptation to embroider on history and re-interpret known events from a different vantage point. Spanish history has been cruel to the Communist Party. Its underground work to maintain resistance to Francoism was not directly rewarded (by the electorate) with a strong parliamentary presence. Instead, they handed it an uneasy role on the margins of institutional power, yet also sidelined from mass-participation movements. The Communist Party suffered from two bitter contradictions: its members felt that 'Against Franco We Struggled Better' (a reworking of the far Right slogan 'With Franco We Lived Better') and its leaders noticed that they had had more influence on a centre-right government than they wielded on a socialist one – in short, that they got on better with their enemies than with their potential allies.

The PCE did not unreservedly deserve its fate, in so far as its past sins were hardly greater than those of other parties on the left and certainly fewer than those of the Francoists. Whatever historians may say in the post-communist era, its is salutary to find that Spanish politicians rarely if ever felt the need to 'blackwash', still less to conduct a witch hunt of the PCE. Some of this may be due to the political class's recognition that Carrillo had been one of the originators of Eurocommunism (despite the fact that he borrowed it from Fernando Claudín after having him expelled from the Party) and shared the merit of having distanced himself from Stalinism as well as the post-Stalinist Soviet leaders. As he reminds us, the PCE recognised that the Soviet Union shared some characteristics with fascist dictatorships, even calling it a socialist version of 'totalitarianism'.

In this and in his dealings with the power elite during the transition, he showed clairvoyance and far-sightedness. Carrillo does a creditable job of reminding us how the PCE's behaviour contributed to getting the transition through some difficult moments. Indeed he makes the bold claim that in April 1977 the PCE held the fate of the transition in its hand, and saved it by not taking up the gauntlet thrown down by the army high command when it criticised the Party's legalisation. If the PCE had refused to stick by its acceptance of the monarchy and had refused to participate in the elections, Carrillo claims that it was very likely that Suárez and the ministers most resolutely in favour of democratisation would have had to resign. Despite this, the flexibility shown by the PCE in giving up the Republican flag and accepting the monarchy did not signal a deeper modernisation of the Party – only the leadership's need to seek an accommodation with Suárez in order to ensure the Party's survival into the democratic era.

Carrillo's point that the Moncloa pacts were the first concrete outcome of consensus is meaningful. He calls them the first written document in which agreement between the opposition and the reformers of the regime was registered, and makes the useful distinction between their agreement and the mere one-sided acquiescence or grudging acceptance of what the other side had done, which characterised the previous stage of transition before the parties' strengths had been put to the test in the first elections. In his view, it was at the Moncloa Palace meetings that the enemies finally buried the hatchet. Equally revealing is the reminder of the contents of the pact: firstly the social section, a series of clearly progressive measures, in fact, a catalogue of gains for the Left. Secondly, the fact that Fraga refused to sign the political section on freedoms. It is a fitting reminder of Alianza Popular's poor democratic credentials at the time, corroborated by the way that several deputies later refused to vote in favour of the Constitution: twelve out of sixteen AP deputies abstained in the Congress vote on the draft, and six still abstained on the final vote in Congress after the draft had been amended in the Senate.

Yet it was Carrillo's refusal to modernise the Party internally, to democratise its structures sufficiently to allow the group of 'renovators' – his true heirs, one could say, in the light of the later evolution of the Italian PCI – to earn their place. This led to the Party's poorest ever showing in the October 1982 election and caused his own resignation a few days later on 6 November and his subsequent political obscurity. By then it was too late for the Party to recover nor hold its own as an electoral force without having to join up with other groups in a Party-coalition. Like so many Communist era leaders, he came to identify himself so strongly with his own leadership that he became convinced the Party could not do without him (Claudín, 1983). How different from the story of the Communists in Italy. Carrillo's touches of bitterness have a point: the result has been the absence of a creditable opposition on the left of the PSOE that would have served to stem its drift to the centre while in government. The Left-of-Left failed to become a genuine voice of the excluded, marginalised and voiceless in Spanish society or to express the concerns of grass-roots activists, non-governmental organisations, campaigning or support groups, but Carrillo also bears some responsibility for this.

Gregorio Peces-Barba's contribution to this volume is of a rather different nature. Given his role in drafting the Constitution, he offers some fascinating insights into the detailed negotiations that lay behind the grand constitutional settlement that was the transition's culmination. His focus is on the Constitution not as a stage in the process, but as the embodiment of the transition as a political style and as a very specific set of outcomes. This focus is justified when one considers that there would have been no lasting, historic value to Suárez's initiatives if they had not led to an enlightened democracy mounted on the stable ground of constitutional consensus.

Peces-Barba reserves most of his criticisms for the regional nationalists. The PNV comes under fire in the transition period for losing interest in the negotiations and not signing up to the constitutional settlement despite the text's recognition of historic Basque rights and its Title VIII setting out the routes to regional autonomy. The PNV is blamed for allowing the non-democratic separatists and terrorists to advance the nationalist cause on their behalf in the 1990s. He decries the tactics of the PNV in what is perceived as its manipulative use of contacts with ETA to use the threat of further violence to bargain for nationalist gains in exchange for temporary ceasefires. This, in Peces-Barba's view, cannot be justified.

It raises again the unmentioned but important issue of the reasons for the PNV's absence from the constitutional drafting committee, and later absence and abstention in the two crucial Congress votes on the draft and final text of the document. The parties to the consensus moved ahead without the PNV in 1978, despite their rhetoric of inclusion. Although the PNV campaigned in favour of the Basque Statute of Autonomy the following year (Gunther, 1986: 40), their initial self-exclusion, whether justified or unjustified, ended up by casting a dark shadow over future developments in the region and has provided the PNV with an eternal alibi for deviating from the conventions of what constitutes legitimate political dissent.

The Catalan nationalists are also robustly criticised for veering towards unconstitutionality in their language policy, since they are perceived as proposing the concept of an exclusive 'own' language to supersede constitutional notions of two co-official languages in the autonomies that boast a linguistic identity.

According to Peces-Barba, a party cannot abdicate from the consensus, which has no 'unilateral exit' and does not admit ongoing haggling or *à la carte* amendments. In his account one can perceive the spectre of the fear of the past, for he is afraid that once one of the parties to the consensus severs its connection to the nucleus of the agreement, out of self-interest, the others may feel able to do the same, and future political stability may be undermined. He warns that the constitutional consensus is 'unavoidably required to keep the peace'.

Miguel Roca, on the other hand, professes not to view the Constitution as a sacrament and offers a distinction between re-negotiating major issues and making small amendments, finding himself agreeable to the latter but not the former. He underlines that achieving consensus involved more than simply recognising pluralism or diversity. It was a process of using meeting-points to construct a shared vision and stake out common ground. While consensus may now be questioned in Spain and a new tendency has emerged to talk up the advantages of an adversarial style of politics, Roca insists consensus was never meant to be a stop-gap answer to a passing situation.

Regarding the Autonomous Communities, he emphasises how the provisions of Title VIII, where the powers that are transferable to the Autonomies seem modest on paper, in the end permitted the greatest process of decentralisation seen in post-war Europe in the seventies and eighties. Their piecemeal development has worked better than expected. Arguing against constitutional reform, Roca maintains that the powers enjoyed by the Autonomous Communities can be increased both through an ambitious, open-minded reading of the Constitution itself without any amendments being necessary. He proposes a way out of the problem by disentangling the mesh of issues currently discussed in Spain under the umbrella of reform: the Senate's functions, Autonomous Community finances and other constitutional defects.

Roca does not shy away from grasping the thorny issue of secession and autonomy 'differentials'. While the Constitution's scribes purposefully made the *nacionalidades* and *regiones* distinction, neither they nor other politicians have so far found an answer to Spain's plurinational reality. He pleads for an understanding of the sensibilities of the historic nationalities, while firmly rejecting their view of the inadequacy of the Constitution in this respect.

The current state of Spanish consensus politics that emerges from these accounts is one of unresolved tension. The possibility is being envisaged that the end of the post-authoritarian consensus has been reached, but the idea that the foundational settlement faces re-negotiation arouses deep misgivings. The feeling as it emerges from these accounts is, in a nutshell, 'let sleeping dogs lie'. Having got the historic dogs of dissent to sleep, not a single one should be woken, lest it should bark. For bark it will, and even bite.

Notes

1 See Coser bibliography in Powell and Robbins, 1984.
2 In some accounts he is considered the symbol around which reconciliation crystallised, and his central situation allowed him to act as an *'instancia reconciliadora'*, almost an institution of reconciliation, in a context where reconciliation meant widening the political spectrum, freedom and pluralism (del Aguila & Montoro, 1984: 134).
3 *Rupturistas* were those demanding a complete break with the past, usually entailing the collapse or resignation of a government and takeover by a provisional government.
4 *Ruptura pactada* is the term most used to sum up the nature of the transition, a prime example of consensus terminology since a negotiated break is a compromise between a gradual reform and a sudden break.
5 An official translation is published by the *Boletín Oficial del Estado*.

References

Claudín, F. *Santiago Carrillo: crónica de un secretario general*, Barcelona: Planeta, 1983.
Coser, L. *The functions of social conflict*, London: Routledge & Kegan Paul, 1956.
Coser, L. 'Consensus' in *Twentieth Century Social Thought*, Oxford: Blackwell, 1994.
Cotarelo, R. (ed) *Transición política y consolidación democrática: España 1975–86*, Madrid: C.I.S., 1992.
Crick, B. *In defence of politics*, revised ed., Harmondsworth: Penguin, 1964.
de Tocqueville, A. *Democracy in America*, Oxford: Oxford University Press, 1946.
del Aguila, R. & Montoro, R. *El discurso político de la transición*, Madrid: C.I.S., 1984.
del Aguila, R. 'La dinámica de legitimidad en el discurso político de la transición' in Cotarelo, R. (ed) *Transición política y consolidación democrática: España 1975-86*, Madrid: C.I.S., 1992.
González, F. (reported by Hernández-Rodicio, A. and Barroso, J.) Madrid: *El País* , 26 September, p.20. 1999.
Higley, J. & Gunther, R. (eds) *Elites and democratic consolidation in Latin America and Southern Europe*, Cambridge: Cambridge University Press, 1995.

Gaviria, M. *La séptima potencia: España en el mundo,* Barcelona: Ediciones B, 1996.

Gómez Puentes, C. 'La transición española: estudio comparativo de las dos últimas constituciones democráticas' in Tussell, J. et al (eds) *Historia de la transición y consolidación democrática en España,* Madrid: UNED & Universidad Autónoma de Madrid, pp.77–88, 1995.

Gunther, R. 'The Spanish Socialist Party: from clandestine opposition to party of government' in Payne, S. (ed.) *The politics of democratic change,* Chicago: Chicago Council on Foreign Relations, pp.8–49, 1986.

Gunther, R. Diamondouros N. & Puhle, H. J. (eds) *Politics of democratic consolidation: Southern Europe in comparative perspective,* Baltimore: Johns Hopkins University Press, 1995.

Heywood, P. 'Governing a new democracy: the power of the Prime Minister in Spain', *West European Politics,* 14: 2, pp.96–115, 1991.

Heywood, P. *The government and politics of Spain,* London: Macmillan, 1995.

Huntington, S. 1992 'How countries democratize', *Political Science Quarterly,* Vol.106/4, pp.579–616, 1992.

Linz, J.J. & Stepan, A., *Problems of democratic transition and consolidation,* Baltimore and London: Johns Hopkins University Press 1996.

Maravall, J.M. *The Transition to Democracy in Spain,* London: Croom Helm, 1982.

Middlemas, K. *Politics in an industrial society,* London, 1979.

Morlino, L. 'Authoritarianism' ch.5 in Beble, A. & Seroka, J. (eds), *Contemporary Political Systems,* Boulder: Lynne Rienner, 1990.

Newton, M. *The institutions of modern Spain : a political and economic guide,* revised ed., 1997.

Osksenberg, M. & Dickson, B.J. 'Origins, processes and outcomes of great political reform' in Rustow, D.A. & Erikson, K.P. ,eds, *Comparative political dynamics,* Harper Collins, 1991.

Potter, D., Goldblatt, D., Kiloh, M. & Lewis, P. *Democratization,* Milton Keynes: The Open University/Polity Press, 1997.

Powell, W.W. & Robbins, R., eds, *Conflict and consensus – Festschrift in honour of L.A.Coser,* New York, The Free Press, 1984.

Preston, P. *The triumph of democracy in Spain,* London: Methuen, 1986.

Preston, P. *La destrucción de la democracia en España,* Madrid: Ediciones Turner, 1978.

Reilly, K. 'Consensus politics' in Bullock, A., Stallybrass, O. and Trombley, S. eds, *Modern Thought,* London: Fontana, 1988.

Rustow, D. 'Transitions to democracy: towards a dynamic model', *Comparative Politics,* Vol.2 No.3, pp.337–363, 1970.

Sassoon, D. *One hundred years of socialism,* London: I.B.Tauris, 1996.

Share, D. *The making of Spanish democracy,* New York: Praeger Press, 1986.

2. Resisting the Dictatorship through Humour

José María Pérez González (*Peridis*)

By profession an architect, José María Pérez González began publishing his cartoons in 1973 in Informaciones and Cuadernos para el Diálogo. Signing as Peridis he joined El País for its launch in 1976. His talent for caricature and sharp political eye – making hundreds of public figures instantly recognisable in a few tiny strokes – brought him wide acclaim and popularity and his strips continue to illustrate the main news for El País today. His published collections of cartoons provide a revealing pictorial history of Spanish democracy. José María Pérez has also been the founder and promotor of a series of training schools (escuelas-taller) for young people in Spain, which he launched in 1985 in his home town of Aguilar de Campoó and developed in other parts of the country.

The very longevity of the Franco dictatorship, with its severe repression of freedom of expression and its state control of the press, forced people to find subtle ways to give vent to their frustrations at the conditions under which they were forced to live. Dictatorship gave a young generation of humorists and political satirists the opportunity to rise to the challenge of penetrating those imposed silences surrounding the regime: its pathetic pretences to imperial glory, its hounding of dissenting voices, its imposition of cruelly low wages, the neglect of the beggar's plight and even its sexual hypocrisies. Later, the very protagonists of the transition to democracy, some of whom are contributing to this memoir, gave me, as a newcomer to the trade, an unending supply of material and pretexts with which to fill my strips over many years. For the opportunity they gave me, I am deeply grateful.

Caricaturing Franco and his ministers was, of course, forbidden in the early period. Yet even in the first decades after the civil war, cartoonists like Tono managed, by resorting to apparently bland images, which did not seem to be having a go at anybody and would therefore get by the censor, to slip in a bit of a social message. So Tono draws a smartly dressed young lady being followed by two admirers. Without compunction she goes up to a policeman and asks him to 'arrest the short one', so as to leave her in the company of the better-looking tall one. At the same time, Tono reminds us just how much arresting on flimsy pretexts was going on. This style I call *humor blanco*, which

—¿No sabe que no se debe pedir?
—Yo no pido. Es que le estoy enseñando la mano.

– Don't you know begging is forbidden?
– I'm not begging, I'm just showing you my hand

really means bland humour, calculated to be inoffensive, but with an underlying message. Another example is the rather pathetic exchange between a beggar and a lady wearing a hat and shawl, which nevertheless suggests all is not well in a country where beggars grovel and the upper classes miss no opportunity to remonstrate with them.

Many humorists were from families that had some experience of the horrors of war. Death, destruction, torture, firing squads, mourning, mutilated limbs, orphans, hunger and beggars were the stuff of everyday life in post-civil war Spain. Such calamities provided the butt and the bite of their jokes. Yet the humour and the images they produced were the culmination of a very Spanish tradition of black humour whose earlier expressions can be traced back to the picaresque novel and can also be found in the work of some of the most celebrated of Spanish painters.

I am reminded of an extraordinary joke which portrays to perfection that old, dark Spain, *la España negra*, seemingly peopled by widows in perpetual mourning. Gila was an excellent exponent of the new genre of black humour, very much in keeping with Spanish tradition. In an early example, we see a visually soft treatment, but with a sting in the tail: two smiling, naive-looking young men stand in a bar in smart clothes, with their arms around each other. But one of them has a wooden leg. Still smiling, he says 'No, I'm not lame; its just that the firing squad did a bad job on me...'.

It is extraordinary to perceive such lack of resentment and self-deprecating humour in the cartoon. It was rumoured that Gila himself had once been up against a firing squad and had escaped the embrace of death through an unexpected stroke of luck. In another cartoon in the same vein,

—No, yo no soy cojo; es que me fusilaron mal...

– No, I'm not lame; its just that the firing squad did a bad job on me...

two soldiers stand chatting. The one, armless, legless and one-eyed, confides to the other 'They were going to invalid me out, but thank God, I've got very good connections'. The word for connections (*agarraderas*) also means 'handgrips', adding a further touch of cruelty.

Today it is really hard to explain the hunger that Spaniards suffered for many years after the war. But Chumy Chúmez does so in a very forceful way when he draws two poor men trundling across the bleak Castillian plain on a windy, snowy day and the one says to the other: 'I'm longing for the summer so that I can only feel hungry'. The cold spell was bound to pass long before enough food appeared – a reminder too, that in the post-war period a fatalistic attitude was the realistic one to have.

To overcome the feeling of tragedy, cartoonists found inspiration in the Spanish picaresque novel, full of incidences of black humour, such as *El Lazarillo de Tormes*[1], *El Buscón don Pablos*[2], and especially in Cervantes's *El Ingenioso Hidalgo Don Quijote de la Mancha*[3]. In all these masterpieces and in many other works of Golden Age literature, the novel or the play's protagonists repeatedly find themselves in an impecunious situation, or simply end up penniless and hungry, and devote all their waking hours and best efforts in trying to avoid its awful consequences. This age-old hunger, whether real or residual, has only recently ceased to be a familiar feeling to countless Spaniards.

They were going to invalid me out, but thank God, I've got very good connections.

Physical handicap was another faithful companion of many Spaniards, often deftly depicted by the great Velázquez (1599–1660), not only in *Las Meninas* [4] (The maids of honour) where the dwarfs Mari Bárbola and Nicolasito accompany the Infanta Doña Margarita. Velázquez returned to the subject of physical deformity in the series of paintings where he depicts the so-called 'freaks' who peopled the Court of the Habsburg dynasty such as the buffoon named Juan de Austria, and the dwarf Don Sebastián de Morra in the painting *The Boy of Vallecas*[5]. So Chumy Chúmez, in sombre mode, draws an elegant bourgeois couple out on a stroll with just a stump of a man pushing himself along in his wheeled cart – but he is on a lead just like a dog. Parodying the regime's paternalist injunction to well-off families to invite a poor person for Christmas dinner, Chumy has them congratulate themselves, 'Not only do we invite a beggar to our table, but we take him for a walk afterwards so he can digest properly'.

Francisco de Goya was undoubtedly the artist whose impact on the Spanish cartoonists has been greatest, both on account of the plastic quality of his art and of the themes found in his work[6]. His two famous paintings of the Madrid uprising against the troops of the French Emperor Napoleon I which had invaded the country in 1807, *El dos de mayo de 1808*[7], depicting the rising itself, and *El tres de mayo de 1808*, portraying the next day's executions, are fundamental in this respect. On the other hand the portrait of Charles IV and his family (*La Familia de Carlos IV*), dating from 1800–1, is a merciless but faithful caricature-portrait of a royal family in their entirety. Not to speak of his series of etchings 'The Caprices' (*Los Caprichos*) and drawings and etchings entitled 'The disasters of war' (*Los desastres de la guerra*) and 'Proverbs, absurdities or dreams' (*Proverbios, disparates o sueños*), which all coldly depict the horrors and perversities which human beings are capable of. A complete expression of these is found in the laconic phrase which forms part of Goya's drawing of the same name 'Reason's sleep engenders monsters' (*El sueño de la razón produce monstruos*) – an observation whose conciseness encapsulates the essence of humour in general and of Spanish humour in particular.

Even closer to the twentieth century, the goya-esque Solana (1886–1945), fond of depicting carnivals, processions and witches' Sabbaths, sombre paintings with a tragic accent, also influenced the post-war generation of cartoonists profoundly, especially through the drawings of his disciple Enrique Herreros. He was the creator of many of the front covers of a key publication, the satirical magazine *La Codorniz* (The Quail). Together with Mihura and Tono they launched the first generation of post-war

Not only do we invite a beggar to our table, but we take him for a walk afterwards so he can digest properly.

cartoonists with what was, after all, the only type of humour permitted: bland, clean, politically uncommitted. But as I said earlier, it served their purpose at the time.

As a political cartoonist, I joined this illustrious group of Spanish humorists rather late, at a time when Mingote was its best known exponent, towards the end of the 1960s and early 1970s. They were fully engaged in the huge task of stripping off the regime's façade and spoofing its omnipresent leaden official language, long since obsolete. They cleverly got round the obstacles put up by the censors and used intelligence as a weapon to share a mutual joke at their oppressors' expense. It would be hard to find any other example in recent history of such a small band of cartoonists battling against the language of a dictatorship with nothing but a sheet of paper, a sharpened pencil and an ingenious mind. Their secret weapon was launching a variety of crypto-languages full of metaphors and *double entendres*, for which they were able to count on the complicity of their readers who relished being able to decipher the hidden meanings of this codified graphic language. This is how Máximo put it in an interview he gave:

> Cartoonists had to find a mode of expression which their accomplices, the readers, could understand but which in a court of law could not be proven to mean what the cartoonist really meant it to mean, although the audience understood it perfectly.

Simply double-Dutch. A nice illustration is Martin Morales' character, the besashed official, justifying the regime's umpteenth refusal to change any of its policies: 'It would

It would be suicidal to undo now what we have spent the last forty years not doing.
By Martin Morales.

I take back what I said, but not what I think.
By Martin Morales.

be suicidal to undo now what we have spent the last forty years not doing'. Or the protester with his banner announcing, 'I take back what I said, but not what I think'.

Recourse to meta-languages became so widespread that they were also used in a twisted way in the official press, leading Gila to confess his despair on returning from one of his long trips to Argentina: 'When I get back to Spain and read the papers, I can't understand a word, but my friends tell me not to be silly, all I have to do is read between the lines. The trouble is, all I see between the lines is blank space!'

The Franco regime endlessly repeated a set of slogans and pet phrases which became increasingly devoid of meaning as time went on, little realising that their hackneyed expressions had become a source of fun to their enemies, who enjoyed using them almost as much as they did. One of the best-known Francoist children's songs boasted the refrain 'Forward I go down imperial highways' (*Voy por rutas imperiales*), oblivious to the notorious absence of roads in Spain, a feature that persisted throughout the whole Franco era. Undeterred, the regime was always 'moving forwards, neither hastening nor tarrying' (*Sin prisas pero sin pausas*) to as yet unsurpassed achievements, which were always 'By land, sea and air' (*Por tierra, mar y aire*) – a reference to the Nationalist victory over the Republicans. Doubts could be banished with a confident, 'The empire will lead us to God' (*Por el imperio hacia Dios*). Any failures were blamed on Jews and masons wrapped into one big 'Judeo-masonic conspiracy' (*La conspiración judeo-masónica*) and total fiascos on 'the enemy, lurking in the shadows, ever ready to pounce' (*El enemigo que agazapado en la sombra sin desmayo*

Instead of a mason in disguise why can't it just be a mosquito? By Forges.

acecha...). No wonder then that the Falangists, after decades in power, still bleated on about 'our pending revolution' (*Tenemos una revolución pendiente*), the one they had never managed to organise.

Some of these clichés are turned around to good effect. Forges made this his trademark, transposing the official-sounding phrases into domestic settings where they looked even more incongruous, and served to strip the legion of Falangist bureaucrats of their pretensions. Where a pyjama-clad husband leaps out of the marital bed to swat a mosquito with sword and shield, readers would have recognised the message: the regime over-reacting to its critics and using excessive force against puny opponents.

Where the lives of their less fortunate fellow Spaniards were concerned, the Francoists could justify any pecuniary meanness with a sententious 'They'll only spend it on wine' (*Para que luego se lo gasten en vino*), and even dismiss dire poverty with the proverbial 'He who does not work does not care to work' (*El que no trabaja es porque no quiere*). The cartoonists' frequent concern with poverty takes issue with these attitudes.

Freedoms continued to be suppressed with the smug 'Let us not confuse liberty with libertinism' (*No hay que confundir libertad con el libertinaje*), trotted out by officialdom whenever the censor was criticised for over-reaching himself. When Franco failed to keep the lid on dissent, this was hailed as an important 'exchange of considerations' (*Tener un contraste de pareceres*), and lauded as proof of openness. These

MINIMUM WAGE
In any case, it would be worse if they were demanding a fair one. By Máximo.

22

leaden refrains with which the public were mercilessly pounded year in, year out, were in turn to take a systematic hammering from the post-war generation of cartoonists, who had lived through the civil war and suffered its aftermath.

By the 1960s, cartoonists were beginning to get published in the newspapers, not just in off-beat magazines. Mingote was an assiduous contributor to *ABC*, and Galindo and Dátile to *Ya*. Máximo was even commenting on low wages and questions of class in *Pueblo*, the newspaper of the official trade union organisation. A boss comments to another as they sprawl on plush sofas in a VIP lounge 'There's nothing more class-ridden than the world of work. I'll bet that 99 per cent of workers are sons of workers.'

Thanks to the Press Law, we can now say 'Yes, but…' to unimportant issues. By Máximo.

The majority of cartoonists made great efforts to get close to their readers, and pushed themselves to find ways to extend the limited boundaries of the Francoist realm of freedom of expression through humour, often getting short shrift from editors and censors. With the new Press and Printing Law of 1966, a 'concession' by Franco's Information Minister, Manuel Fraga, pre-emptive censorship disappeared. Instead a permanent sword of Damocles hung over newspaper editors' heads.

In another, a scriptwriter who goes beyond the pale gets his script rejected with the advice: 'Follow the Americans' example: they make films criticising their customs and institutions, don't they? Write me a script criticising customs and institutions in America'.

The daily *Madrid*, in which Chumy Chumez drew some hard-hitting stuff, as seen below, was the paper which most endured the rigours of the new situation. After several suspensions it was forced to close and later fold completely, but not after publishing a landmark editorial. Commenting on General De Gaulle's withdrawal from politics after losing his referendum, the editorial under the heading *Retiring on Time* portrayed his decision as exemplary, in a not-so-veiled allusion to the ageing Franco. Though not mentioned by name, of course, he was clearly the target of the article. But he was not to take the hint.

For all these reasons the popularity of these cartoonists among the general public in those days was huge, so much so that the collected volumes of their cartoons sold

Mind what you are thinking. There's a microphone in one of the barrels. By Chumy Chúmez.

hundreds of thousands of copies, becoming the mainstay of not a few struggling publishers. One would have to go all the way back to the time of Bagaría in *El Sol* – the best known Spanish cartoonist before the civil war, who died in exile – to find someone as popular as Forges or Perich in the 1970s. Viewers of Forges's small Francoist in a large marital bed, depicted as lacking in sexual prowess in contrast to his public power, would gain satisfaction from seeing the petty tyrant so diminished.

*I'm not asking the impossible…
just imagine I am the people… By Forges.*

The publication of the satirical magazine *Hermano Lobo* (Brother Wolf) was the occasion for open rejoicing. People congregated expectantly around their local kiosk, waiting for the latest issue, sharing the feeling of complicity between readers, and then devoured its contents. Sadly, the rivalry generated by the launch of *Por Favor* (If You Please) in Cataluña, divided the small band of humorists into two, splitting the readers as well. In the end it led to the disappearance of both publications. But thanks to *Hermano Lobo*, for at least a short while readers were able to enjoy the work of a whole group of humorists at their peak. Forges, Chumy Chumez, Máximo, Perich, Gila, Summers, filled the inside pages and took turns to appear on the weekly cover. New talent was taken on board too, such as OPS who made a big impact, and now publishes in the daily *El País* under the signature *El Roto*. That period also saw the appearance of Martin Morales, some of whose biting critique of officialdom appears here.

Caricaturing politicians directly had been out of bounds for obvious reasons. I myself got a break with my first cartoons in the daily *Informaciones* edited by Jesús de la Serna in about 1973, and later I was lucky enough to join the *El País* team from the time it was launched in May 1976 with Juan Luis Cebrián as editor. Later I was amazed to find out how much I owed to Bagaría, without realising it. I first heard of him from friends returning from exile – specifically the veteran socialist, later Senator, José Prat. It was a small miracle to discover that across the enormous distance of half a century separating me from Bagaría, and even across very different personal circumstances, there could be such likenesses in the way we express ourselves. His love of line, the sobriety of his sketches, and the use of symbols to enhance and extend the possibilities of the visual language – with Bagaría I share a belief that caricature brings out the inner physiognomy of things and people. Cartoonists extract the essential traits from their subject – or at least I believe that to be the real challenge: to capture the person's character with the minimum strokes of the pen. But not any strokes – it is not a question of elongating a nose or of holding up this or that facial or body feature to ridicule. It is all to do with synthesising traits, eliminating the unessential to pare it down to their soul, so to speak, and incorporating a psychological sketch with the minimum graphic resources. In the same way as a playwright does when creating a character, cartoonists underline each person's main traits. Curiously, after the cartoonist has extracted a person's real traits, it is they, the subject, who will be burdened for the rest of their life with their caricature – that is, as long as the cartoonist gets it right...

In my daily strip I nailed the Communist Party leader Santiago Carrillo as a cheeky devil forever trying to leave the 'lowlife' of the public drain hole; the conservative 'longlife' politician Manuel Fraga as overweening ambition dressed up in a thousand disguises; Adolfo Suárez (Prime Minister from 1976–81), the man who made it in politics by first scrambling to the top of the column of power; Alfonso Guerra, deputy leader of the PSOE and deputy Prime Minister under González, as the biting and pitiless busy bee; Leopoldo Calvo Sotelo (Prime Minister from 1981–2) as a sphinx, who then leaves his post without anyone being able to decipher his message. For his part, in my strip Felipe González managed after many years in power to occupy the top of Suárez's column, and I've drawn him as a pharaoh figure in many of his attributes. But in the end he had to get off his pedestal, so to speak, and pass on the inevitably lonely pillar of power to José María Aznar, for him to handle it like an executive toy, a mere plaything.

The cartoonist extracts from each character their particular essence, like a favourite perfume which becomes their distinguishing feature. Sometimes the cartoonist only manages to get a whiff, but from whiff to whiff and person to person, gradually the essence is picked up and each politician's traits are delineated. While each can be individually identified, if all the essences are made to mingle a single over-arching aroma is created which identifies each and every cartoonist. In this way we can even see ourselves reflected in our caricatures, represented in each and every politician – with the only difference that they openly display the traits which most of the time the cartoonist prefers to dissemble.

And finally, as a further illustration that nature really does imitate art, I would like to mention a strip of mine, published in *El País* in April 1977, about Carlos Arias Navarro, Franco's loyal friend, appointed Prime Minister from 1973–6. Arias, who had vowed to be the faithful executor of Franco's political testament, later took the step of announcing that he would actually *stand for election* to the Senate, as a Popular Alliance candidate. I used to draw him making metaphorical visits to Franco's tomb in the Valley of the Fallen

| I'M STANDING FOR THE SENATE WITH POPULAR ALLIANCE | FOR LOVE OF SPAIN | AND TO SERVE THE KING | IN THAT CASE, FORGET IT! * |

* *The voice off can be the King's – Arias had served him poorly the year before and had been dismissed – or Franco voicing his disapproval of Arias' plans. By Peridis.*

to offer him explanations of his actions or to ask for his opinion. In order to show up the real internal contradictions for a convinced authoritarian like Arias Navarro to try to become democratically elected, I drew the whole Popular Alliance leaders (with Fraga in the centre) carved in the stone of Franco's memorial, as if hewn from the same rock, with Arias emerging from Franco's funerary chamber to announce his candidature – an inauspicious move as it turned out. Imagine my surprise when I found out that this was exactly what Arias used to do, visit the Valley of the Fallen to 'ask' Franco for advice and even for forgiveness for not being able to halt the march of time![8]

I would like to take this opportunity to pay homage to my fellow cartoonists, for their brave and wonderful work, which is increasingly appreciated as years go by, and for their contribution to freedom and democracy in Spain. They took risks and experienced moments of anguish, but by drawing on their own intelligence and tolerance in equal measures they helped to make the transition to democracy in Spain easier, and above all, more fun.

Notes

1 The life of Lazarillo of Tormes, his fortunes and adversities, 1554, author unknown, a great example of classical Spanish prose.
2 Written in 1626 by Quevedo, a violent satire of the society of the time and outstanding example of the genre.
3 Miguel de Cervantes (1547–1616) published the first part of *The Adventures of the Ingenious Nobleman Don Quixote of La Mancha* in 1605, and completed it ten years later. The apogee of Spanish renaissance literature.
4 1656, Museo del Prado, Madrid.
5 c.1645, Museo del Prado, Madrid. While he was enlisted as the official portraitist to the royal family (Philip IV) and the higher nobility, Velásquez made a series of studies of madmen and buffoons around 1645 (Gudiol, J. *The Arts of Spain*, London: Thames and Hudson, 1964, p.266–7).
6 Francisco de Goya y Lucientes (1746–1828) witnessed the crushing of the rebellion in Madrid, some of it at first hand (Chabrun, J.F., *Goya*, London: Thames and Hudson, 1965: 166).
7 Also known respectively as The Charge of the Mamelukes and The Execution of the Defenders of Madrid, painted in 1814.
8 Arias admitted frequent visits to commune with Franco in an interview with the journalist Pedro J. Ramírez (Preston, 1986: 118).

Translation by Monica Threlfall.
All footnotes by the editor.

3. Adolfo Suárez's Stewardship of the Transition – A memoir

Alberto Aza

Alberto Aza was Adolfo Suárez's chef de cabinet *from 1977–81, with the civil service rank of Director-General. Born in 1937 in Spanish Morocco, he graduated from the Spanish School of Diplomacy in 1963. After postings in Africa and southern Europe, he returned to Madrid at the start of the transition. After Adolfo Suárez's resignation as Prime Minister, Alberto Aza became Spain's Permanent Observer to the Organisation of American States based in Washington D.C., followed by Ambassador to Mexico in 1990. From 1992–1997 he was Spanish Ambassador to London, before returning to the Ministry of Foreign Relations in Madrid.*

I have a big surprise for you. By Peridis

This turned out to be a prescient think bubble: Suárez's politics were a surprise to all – Ed.

There must have been countless rounds of speculation about the future of Spain after Franco. I think it came to be an obsession not only in political circles but even more so for ordinary Spaniards like me. I was one of the pessimists. Playing this guessing game in Rome in 1975, I placed my bets on a military outcome and wagered that the leading role would be played, as in Greece, by the *colonels* because I refused to accept that there were any *generals* intelligent enough to take power.

In this jolly frame of mind I completed my first ten years of foreign service and returned to the Ministry of Foreign Affairs at the end of that critical year, 1975, just weeks before Franco's death. Alberto Cortina was Foreign Minister at that time. I went to work in the minister's private office and, from my small patch, I could see the unwholesome spectacle of Franco's system gradually rotting from the inside. The way in which the Sahara crisis was dealt with was a good example of this.[1] The first government of the monarchy was dubbed 'continuist' (*continuista*), following in Franco's footsteps.[2] Perhaps the repeated readings of Franco's political testament in the media contributed to a growing fear that nothing would change under the restored monarchy.

I remained in the Foreign Minister's private office under a new minister, José María de Areilza, who was a monarchist and a conservative but also considered to be liberal-minded. He took the first steps towards gaining international recognition for the new monarchy, firstly with the USA, through the signing of the Hispano-North American Agreement and, later, with other European countries. A few weeks later I transferred from the Foreign Minister's private office to the ministry's public relations unit, the OID (Office of Diplomatic Information), and in this role I accompanied Areilza on many of his trips to European capitals.

Let me first explain that Areilza was promoting the most inadequate and incomplete plan for democracy, in which elections would eventually be held for an assembly which would, in turn, decide which parties of the Left would be allowed to stand in some future election. Areilza was doubtful whether the Socialist Party would be permitted to take part in the process and asserted that under no circumstances would it be possible for the Communist Party to do so. At the time there was a widespread fear in Europe that a leftist regime would come to power in Spain, especially after the Revolution of the Carnations in Portugal.[3] European politicians did not bat an eyelid as they listened to Areilza and generally took it for granted that the Communists would be excluded from the political party scene, as had happened in quite a few democratic Western nations.

The space for democratic change was indeed limited in these circumstances. The *aperturista* speeches[4] intimating changes yet using Francoist language, made by politicians such as Suárez who themselves had been part of the dictatorship, seemed to me to be neither credible nor encouraging. When Arias resigned I wondered whether Areilza could be the *aperturista* candidate for Prime Minister and it came as a bombshell when I heard that it was Adolfo Suárez who had been chosen by the King on 5 July 1977.[5] At the height of the summer on a Costa Brava beach, Suárez's promises of political change sounded good on television but I still did not believe them. I was convinced that it was a trick and that any change would be engineered so that everything stayed the same.

The new Foreign Minister, Marcelino Oreja, kept me on at the Office of Diplomatic Information (OID). I should explain that the Prime Minister's Cabinet Office at that time had no traditions to fall back on and therefore lacked any support structure of its own, so the OID handled the press when the Prime Minister travelled abroad, as it did when the King and Queen went on their visits. It therefore handled the new Prime Minister's visits to Mexico and the United States and I was put in charge of relations with the press. Despite this I had actually seen the Prime Minister only on television and did not meet Suárez personally until spring 1977.

On that trip to the USA, on board the noisiest Armed Forces DC8 you could imagine, the members of the so-called 'support entourage' had a working meeting with the Prime Minister. Suárez straight away said 'let's talk politics'. It was my political road to Damascus, more because I believed in what I had already seen rather than believing in what I had yet to see. While the government's plans had seemed disordered to me before, now they seemed coherent. It is true that at that time there had already been crisis points in the reform process, as over the approval by referendum of the Law for Political Reform in December 1976, for example, when the opposition called for abstention. I too had abstained, although I had gone to the polls with my wife who voted in favour (she is sharply intuitive and has always had more common sense than me). I had yet to understand that the changes proposed[6] were part of an overall plan and were not being improvised on a day to day basis. I needed to be convinced that this time the words – the rhetoric – were to be consistent with a real conviction that democracy for the whole nation was Suárez's objective.

The conversation in the DC8 lasted hours, and Suárez the charmer was overwhelming. I became convinced that Spain was now entering the final lap towards real democracy. At the end of the trip, at the Embassy in Washington, Suárez turned to Marcelino Oreja, the Foreign Minister and said, 'I'll take this man with me to the Moncloa [The Prime Minister's official residence], if he accepts'. Turning to me, he asked 'What do you say?' I replied 'Before this trip, I would never have worked with you. Now, I will accept anything that's going.' He even offered me a choice: Head of the Prime Minister's Private Office, or Prime Minister's Spokesman. I took the former. When I met up with some friends in New York who had connections with one of the socialist leaders, Enrique Tierno[7], and related my experience, they were amazed at my conversion.

Believe me, it is not my aim to give a personal history as if I were a retired general recounting his battles. I only mention this incident because I believe that I was not the only one in Spain who felt this way, among those of us who were convinced that change had to come from below and had to be driven by the Left. Possibly it was this idea of change from below and from the Left that scared Spanish society following Franco's death. Spanish society was seeking tranquillity in freedom, security in democracy, change but not trauma. In short, people were scared of the ghosts of the past and of a political vacuum. Francoism without Franco was not viable since it had been a personal regime. The transition took on board these feelings. The instruments of change were moderation, centrism and reform based on existing authoritarian laws.

I arrived at Moncloa Palace a few days before the first democratic elections were held, but I played no role in them. My main concern in my new job was to find out where the functions and powers of the Prime Minister's Office, of which I was now the Head, had got to. The support administration for a democratic Prime Minister had to have a formal role somewhere. I was stunned when I discovered that no such office formally existed and that my high-sounding department comprised two efficient secretaries and myself. And during the years I was in the job, the law of bureaucracy that says that whoever has power only gives it up unwillingly proved to be effective. The structures and staff members of the office were constantly changed to suit the Prime Minister's needs, which varied according to political priorities or to internal tensions within the government or the party. In any case, I never abandoned the idea that the ideal Prime Minister's Office should be small, and should not become a second Cabinet. Likewise, it should ensure that the ministries were accessible to the Prime Minister and worked for him too, and not exclusively for the political survival of their specific minister, however legitimate this might be. The scarcity of resources was outrageous. The government had no official spokesperson, having abolished the Ministry of Information[8]. I put together a rudimentary unit in the Prime Minister's Office that was able to handle media enquiries. The person who took over and endured this responsibility was the speech writer, Fernando Onega.

The Elections of 15 July 1977: An Unforgettable Day

The avenues of democracy were wide open after the election, but opening the way is not the same as going down it – much less so when one travels down the road before it is even paved. Nearly everything had still to be accomplished, though it could all be summed up in a few words: the goal of the political reform was to establish and consolidate a modern parliamentary monarchy. Up until that time, Spanish society could be credited with having taken a major step towards democracy with the elections, but there had been no constitutional endorsement either of the new system or of any new social model. So the priority of the first democratic government was to give Spain a constitution.

The government took steps to bring matters to a quick conclusion by proposing a short constitution. One of its advantages was thought to be that it would soon fill the void relating to the monarchy as the form of state, which lacked formal endorsement. But the opposition rejected this proposal as they considered it to be an imposition from above. The opposition aspired to be much more than just a chorus to the government, especially since the Socialist Party (PSOE) had managed to win sufficient votes to be the alternative for power.[9]

Working with *all* the political forces, that is, creating a consensus, had to be the dominant approach in any constitutional debate. The new Constitution turned out to be longer than initially planned and reflected a number of the parties' demands as contained in some of their electoral manifestoes. In any case, once the Constitution was drafted, the government was satisfied that it would survive any change of government and that it would break our country's traditional constitutional precariousness.[10] Spain's 'model of society', a term much loved by the government and the Prime Minister, took shape as a compromise between the Right and the Left, as understood at the time, of course. Spain had to be a monarchy, a democracy and a social market economy. Both the Prime Minister's will to be progressive and social pressures clearly left their imprint. The Constitution also recognised national diversity within the unity of Spain. Spanish was the official language, but other languages would be recognised and legitimately taught.

The Basque Nationalist Party (PNV) did not support the Constitution. Their parliamentary representatives had attempted to have their policy of a 'Pact with the Crown' accepted as the basis for their relationship with the Spanish state. The Prime Minister studied the draft text of the Constitution down to the smallest detail in order to avoid any last minute ambiguity that might slip through the final negotiations in the committee drafting the Constitution. The proof that the consensus approach proved fruitful lies in the fact that it is precisely in the areas where consensus was not achieved that many of the difficulties of Spanish political life have subsequently arisen.

The referendum of 6 December 1978 to approve the Constitution brought this cycle to an end and led the country to fresh elections in March 1979 and to a second government headed by Adolfo Suárez and his Union of the Democratic Centre (UCD).

Problems on all Fronts

1. The Forces of Reaction

The major difficulty throughout the transition was trying to get a new Constitution implemented and governing in a spirit of democracy, while lacking the supporting elements that a structured and consolidated democracy usually provides to those in power. New structures had to be put in place and consolidated at the same time as the government was being opposed, despite its unquestionable electoral weight, by the Spanish establishment, the de facto powers as they were known. The Spanish establishment had not thrown in its lot with democracy. Large sectors of the business world opposed economic reforms as basic as a modern tax system in which taxes would actually be paid out of a sense of responsibility, consisting not just of payroll taxes but income, inheritance and capital gains taxes too. The financial sector was opposed to the deregulation and opening up of the banking sector to foreign competition. Foreign banks finally came to Spain in stages, with restrictions, and only after a great tug-of-war which led the Prime Minister to threaten to take control of the banks which opposed the government's policy. When Suárez and Giscard first met in Paris, the French President asked him what he would do if the banks opposed international openness and was astonished to hear the reply 'nationalise them'.

2. The Church

By 1978 there could no longer be any doubt that the state was constitutionally secular or that other religions could be freely practised. Furthermore, the influence of the Catholic church and the size of some of its congregations were falling, in some cases because of moral conflicts over such matters as divorce, and in others, because of its grip over education. A sector of the Catholic hierarchy found it difficult to assimilate the introduction of divorce, the expansion of state education and other losses of privilege, and fed the Vatican stories of their anxieties, without comprehending that one of the key elements for a peaceful transition to democracy was precisely to accept and forget the past. The laws on divorce and the management of schools were approved by parliament but irretrievably divided the governing UCD's parliamentary group. This split was the first battle won in the internal struggle to push the parliamentary group towards the right, but the ultimate victor was the PSOE. From that time onwards, whenever a consensus was needed to pass an 'organic' (highest order) law[11] which, under the Constitution, requires an absolute majority on the amended draft in the lower house (the Congress of Deputies), negotiations were as tough within the UCD itself as they were with the PSOE, and sometimes tougher.

3. The Armed Forces

For almost one hundred and fifty years, the armed forces had been the guarantor of the power and influence of Spanish conservatism and its long-standing predominance over political life. The armed forces were bloated and top-heavy, had played no part in any international armed conflicts[12], had few resources and, having become deeply politicised following their victory in 1939, their upper echelons remained a redoubt of Francoism, with rare exceptions. It was difficult for them to accept the radical political changes that had brought the recognised enemies of Franco's so-called crusade straight into the Congress of Deputies. For them the legalisation of the Communist Party (PCE) was like a nightmare come true and their visible presence in parliament continued to exasperate the armed forces.[13] Communists were not the only 'enemies of Spain', so too were the socialists who still claimed to be Marxist and against the American bases – all leftists in any case. So the government of the UCD was equally upset, for it not only allowed these people to be politically active but was even relaunching the experiment with federalisation against which the army had fought for the sake of the country's unity. Spain was disintegrating, Spain was breaking up, they feared.

The Suárez government was included as an enemy because it was determined to reform the armed forces, their strategic objectives and their promotion systems, and above all, to put an end to the military's independence and make them subordinate to civilian power. The government was right, of course, but the armed forces were strong. There was almost constant tension. Defiant remarks flew backwards and forwards. Well-known names hid behind anonymous, collective statements calling for action on the part of reactionary forces. Some newspaper editors permitted publication of such articles and, worse still, were ready to allow attempts to manipulate the institution of the Crown. They spread anxiety and made the government waste energies which could have been expended on more constructive tasks. All this culminated on one wretched, deplorable day in February 1981, when a sector of the army and the Civil Guard rose up against the government.[14]

4. Terrorism

Terrorism, particularly on the part of ETA, also contributed to the unrest within the armed forces and the security forces and to bolster the reactionary sectors, kindling fellow feeling between the extremist Fuerza Nueva[15] and some military groups. All wrapped themselves in the flag of a patriotism that was past its sell-by date.

Often, days at the Moncloa Palace became an agonising wait in case a phone call came from the Ministry of the Interior to say that some terrorist act had taken place, generally with casualties from the armed forces, the police or Civil Guard. The terrorist attacks inflicted by GRAPO[16] and ETA everywhere were destabilising, but those in the Basque Country (Euskadi) had a particular resonance. They had a political effect directly linked to the demands for autonomy and independence made by various sectors of the Basque population which, in turn, spread to other regions such as Catalonia and – often forgotten these days – the Canary Islands. Terrorism provided extra ammunition for the reactionary forces. Who can doubt that ETA's aim was to provoke a reactionary response, if not a coup, in order to generate political reasons to justify their existence, just as they had done in the Franco era. The end to terrorism required a police solution but also a political one, but the political solution stoked up the feelings of the reactionary groups and plotters – a vicious circle.

5. The Autonomous Communities

Whilst moving from a totalitarian state to a democratic state is like swimming with the current, moving from a centralised to a decentralised state is like being pushed and pulled by several currents flowing in different directions. It was left to popular sovereignty to solve the problem of the constitutional integration of the regions and nationalities of Spain in a way that would repay a debt to Spanish history – albeit recent, nineteenth-century history. The task would prove almost intractable.

All the pieces of the puzzle had to be fitted together. The beginning of a regional solution was first sought in 1977 with an amnesty, followed by recognition of the Catalan Generalitat.[17] Its leader, Josep Tarradellas returned to Spain, a decentralising constitution was drafted creating autonomous communities and the Catalan Statute of Autonomy was negotiated. The Catalan precedent sought to demonstrate that any rejection of Catalan nationalism was now a thing of the past, that a working relationship between the centre and the periphery was feasible and that central government had confidence in Catalan wisdom (*seny*) and in the conservative nature of Spain's most economically powerful region, a society that was unlikely to turn to violent nationalism. Neither should it be forgotten that Catalonia, almost uniquely among nationalists, offered an interlocutor – someone the government could talk to. This was clear from the start with Josep Tarradellas and has remained so with Jordi Pujol. I believe the Catalan exercise was a success for both sides. In spite of this, the Right, even the parliamentary Right represented by Popular Alliance (AP), did not share our point of view and their leader Manuel Fraga made this clear in heated contributions both inside parliament and outside.

But the Basque question had little in common with the Catalan experience, for which it was only a distant reference point. In the Basque provinces, nationalism and violence appeared to go hand in hand in different ways: from the support given to the armed struggle by the two ETAs, the political/military wing and the military wing, to the ambiguous condemnations of terrorist acts by Basque parties with parliamentary representation, even the Basque Nationalist Party (PNV). The PNV has regularly swung between taking full part in the national political game, as the Catalans have done, to making tactical appearances as a sidelined but not completely disinterested actor.

The state inherited from the Franco years was, paradoxically, extremely weak. I became aware of the Spanish army's limited firepower during the days of Morocco's 'Green March' into Spanish Saharan territory in 1975. But what was important in dealing with the Basque problem was the lack of resources available to the police force. There was a flagrant lack not only of any intelligence network that could function in a democracy, but even of human resources. It has never been fully understood just how impecunious the Spanish state was. Not even the anti-riot squads were trained or equipped for their new tasks in a free state. The mistakes made during repressive operations, even if they could be excused given the facts to hand, provided a pretext for the extreme nationalists to denounce the unpopular police and an excuse for the rest of the nationalist groups to sit on the fence in the face of local opinion.

I believe that the only issue that could seriously have threatened our path during the transition was the political and terrorist problem in the Basque Country. Police successes inflamed the nationalists and terrorist successes inflamed the reactionaries. Basque casualties stoked up Basque nationalism, non-Basque casualties stoked up right-wing patriotism and fed ordinary Spaniards' incomprehension. They would have given way to counterproductive anti-Basque feeling if the government had not demonstrated a certain political shrewdness in its actions.

The negotiation of the Basque Statute of Autonomy in 1979 was evidence of the tact with which the UCD government dealt with the situation in the Basque Country, principally because it refused to present the Statute as its own work, leaving the Basque negotiating team to take the credit, particularly Carlos Garaicoechea, the then PNV leader. He went to Madrid on the morning when the Statute was supposed to be formalised, almost under duress as he had taken leave owing to the death of a much-loved relative. This allowed him to present the Statute as a triumph for the Basques, making it more acceptable to public opinion in Euskadi.

6. *The Economy*

The state of the economy in no way helped the transition process. It would have been infinitely easier to concentrate on political reform in a period of rising standards of living, an upturn in the business cycle and macro-economic indicators approaching those of the surrounding countries. The inflation rate at the time would today terrify the calmest stock exchange traders. The second oil crisis created an uneasiness in the financial world that extended to the general public. In the same way that there was a danger that ordinary people would simply identify terrorism with the arrival of democracy, democracy and economic malaise could also be linked. In some ways, the very seriousness of the situation helped consensus-building among all the parties and trade union confederations to reach the broad political agreement known as the Moncloa Pacts. That this national 'summit' was even held was an achievement which the Prime Minister, once again, decided not to exploit, so that the opposition could consider it to be everyone's success. The PSOE, for example, only agreed to attend the talks at their final stages. González did not want to give the government any reason for claiming a success. The PSOE had grown since the 1977 election, was already intent on victory at the next one and viewed the Prime Minister as a target to be weakened. Ajuriaguerra, the PNV representative at the talks, had to leave soon after they had started because of some terrorist attack. Nonetheless the Moncloa Pacts were an enormous boost for the country and also for the government. Structural adjustment policies and the modernisation of the financial system were put in place. These were the first steps towards modernising the economy during the transition – yet another success for the politics of consensus.

Suárez's Role in Consensus-building

After the first elections in 1977, the UCD as the party of government had to change into something more than an association of small groups, like it had been in the run-up to the elections. But its life as a cohesive party proved to be short-lived. I believe that the Party's success, with two election victories, made the leaders of the political families within the UCD complacent. They lost sight of the fact that Suárez exercised a presidential style of leadership, that the election campaigns had been waged on the strength of the leader's electoral pull, and that the UCD without Suárez would cease to be an electoral success and might even fail to survive an electoral defeat. The question, in fact, is whether it was ever a real party.

As for the opposition, the PSOE had achieved unexpected results in 1977 and believed that they were almost assured of victory in the 1979 elections. Their failure in 1979 forced the Party leadership to put in place a strategy to stop a third socialist defeat which would, ultimately, have destroyed the image of their leader, Felipe González. The first prong of this strategy consisted of attempts to persuade some members of parliament on the centre-left of the UCD to defect to the Socialist parliamentary group. A first attempt had already taken place before September 1979, and would end up contributing to the disintegration of the UCD. The second prong was focused on destroying Suárez himself, a task to which the media contributed very effectively.

Paradoxically, while the Socialists were attacking the UCD and the government, the Prime Minister was working intensely to convert the PSOE into a viable alternative for power. Suárez promoted González's moderate image among political groups who saw reds under every bed, and supported the rebuilding of the Socialist's trade union confederation, UGT, to enable it to compete with the pro-Communist confederation, Workers' Commissions.[18] Trade union reform therefore was not only a logical part of Spain's democratic development, but also played a part in the government's plans, complementing the moderate approach which was essential for a change of government to occur without trauma in Spain.

Foreign Policy

I will now turn to the foreign policy of the Centrist governments to which I contributed. Our links with the countries which had had no relations with the Franco regime – such as Mexico, Israel and parts of Eastern Europe – had to be re-established through diplomatic recognition. The new Spanish institutions had to be accepted internationally. Spain had to take advantage of its transformation to place itself at the heart of Europe. At the same time it had to weather the problems that the second oil crisis had inflicted on Spaniards' daily needs. Threatened by terrorism, our democracy had to consider its domestic security to achieve consolidation.

Marcelino Oreja carried out the tireless task of presenting the monarchy to the international community. The same purpose was served by the Prime Minister's overseas trips and especially by the King and Queen's visits. Western governments had to be persuaded that the process begun during the transition was a firm and solid undertaking, with a modern, Western parliamentary monarchy. This was the message to be passed on to the embassies with the aim of reducing the time we had to wait to be accepted into the 'Western Club'. They had to be persuaded that Spanish stability was guaranteed, which was the same as saying, in its widest possible sense, that security in Europe would be reinforced. The significance of our entry to the Council of Europe, for example, was far greater than the Council's own ranking amongst European organisations, but it represented an acknowledgement of, and confidence in, the future of the Spanish process. The outcome of our constitutional process strongly confirmed the message which our future European partners had already heard. From that moment on, the path towards the European Community and NATO was cleared.

The European Community application had unanimous support in parliament. It was therefore an easy and welcome decision that put us on the same level as other developed countries in democratic Europe, a Europe that acted as a political model and as a stimulus for our domestic process of democratisation. The membership conditions would take a long time to negotiate, but support from the parties and the public kept the spirits of the negotiators high even during difficult times. Let me say that I believe that Spain has always had a European team of which Spaniards can feel proud.

If there was consensus for entry to the European Community, there was none for membership of NATO. Neither the Communist Party nor the Socialist Party supported it. In spite of the fact that our future potential allies were in favour of our joining NATO, the Suárez government decided that a decision of such significance could only be successful if decided *by consensus*. It took the view that it would have been absurd if, having joined on a majority decision with the support of conservative, national and regional parties, a future socialist government would later leave NATO, also on a majority decision, as González was threatening to do.[19] Contrary to what has been said, it was not the case that Suárez or some members of his team were anti-American. He was no simpleton and far from being a political novice. Government circles had noticed the almost imperceptible changes that were taking place in some sectors of the PSOE which presaged a softening of their opposition to NATO membership. At heart, I believe that the PSOE breathed a sigh of relief on the day the Suárez's successor Leopoldo Calvo Sotelo took the decision to apply for membership of NATO. The government's excellent control of political timing contributed to resolving the dilemma entangling the Socialist Party. North Americans and German social-democrats took on the job of trying to persuade the PSOE to shift its anti-NATO stance. It was settled in a referendum that surprised both the Right and the Left because the González government urged the public to vote yes to remaining in NATO, albeit with conditions.[20]

Collaboration with countries abroad was desperately sought in order to make up for the shortcomings of the Spanish intelligence services in the struggle against ETA. Help was sought from Israel, the United States, the United Kingdom, France, and in addition, the government sought to neutralise the support given to terrorist activities from the countries where it was thought there might be training camps. The UCD government was accused of having Third-World sympathies but the public did not realise that, in its relations with the PLO, Cuba, or the Polisario Front, the government was not only seeking coherence for our policy, given the conflicts in the Middle East, the Caribbean or North Africa, but was also seeking to verify the existence of aid to ETA or the MPAIC[21] in order to eliminate it. This has been forgotten today though it was part of our diplomatic activity for many years. The point is that the quite widely held pre-1981 view that we were not joining NATO because non-alignment interested us more, was wrong, even though the USSR would have preferred us to choose non-alignment.

The efforts made by the government to seek France's cooperation in alleviating our problems were part of this strategy of enrolling the help of friendly nations. There is little that can give me greater satisfaction than the fact that we managed to enlist France to fight against ETA. But I have to say that the help provided by France at the time was insufficient[22], and somewhat insensitive to the difficulties and risks of destabilisation that terrorism could have caused in Europe if there had been a reactionary backlash in Spain.

Democratisation gave our foreign policy some ace cards in Latin America. Our relationship with that area was a priority for Spain and it grew in significance. Our aim was to help Spanish-speaking countries to make a peaceful transition from military dictatorships to democratic systems. The Spanish model of transition offered exemplary though not decisive support to the movements for democratisation in Latin America, in addition to assistance provided by some of the member-parties of the UCD to like-minded parties in those countries. All in all, the process of democratisation and the work undertaken by Spanish diplomacy succeeded in changing Spain's image abroad, laying the foundations for the still ongoing process of raising its international profile.

Suárez's Resignation

My account of the main events and difficulties of Adolfo Suárez's government go some way towards explaining the reasons behind the crisis in the UCD following his resignation as Prime Minister in January 1981. The only thing left to complete the picture would be to examine the divisions within the UCD and the reappearance of its factions, but this would involve lengthy explanations of the excessive prominence sought by the various faction leaders, dubbed 'the barons'. Briefly and succinctly, I believe that it was the UCD's reluctance to go down the road of becoming a coherent single party that prevented it from realising its potential. Its power centre, the government, always had the upper hand and sought to radically reform Spain by means of consensus and moderation. But representatives of contradictory lines of thought had been brought together in the UCD parliamentary group. These acted to defend interests other than those of the Party, falling in with unstructured pressure groups who were trying to slow down the rhythm of change. No sooner had democracy been recovered, than the short-sighted members of the political class, lacking a clear understanding of statehood, played their cards – their ambitions for power – as if democracy had already been consolidated. Suárez graphically defined the situation by comparing democracy to a glass ball being tossed around from one politician to another, confident that if they dropped it Suárez would jump up and catch it before it hit the ground. Both the UCD barons and the PSOE played this game. In fact, the crisis within the UCD was an elite crisis at the highest levels of the parliamentary group, not at the level of the rank and file or the electorate.

As to Adolfo Suárez's resignation, there is no reason to dream up outlandish stories of military threats or invitations from high level institutions in order to explain it. His weariness with UCD infighting and the 'baronial' behaviour of the faction leaders is explanation enough. Suárez's resignation speech can only be interpreted one way. The famous paragraph on the need to 'avoid democracy becoming a short interval' in Spanish history was due to the original drafting of the text written by Pepe Meliá, who opted to include this phrase because it was one of Suárez's constant refrains.

The disgraceful attack on parliament and its occupation on 23 February 1981 by a detachment of civil guards showed once again that democracy trusted the outgoing Prime Minister to once more catch the fragile glass ball of democracy before it hit the ground. The attempted coup re-kindled past fears, that same fear that had contributed to the success of the political reform process. After only a few but intense years of experience, millions of Spaniards now massively demonstrated their commitment to democracy and the Crown steadfastly carried out its role as the guarantor of the constitutional order by moving to dismantle the coup.

Consensus

After two decades of democracy the political cycle of transition and consolidation had been fulfilled by the experience of a socialist government. The renewal of the Conservative Party and its coming to power in 1996, began a new cycle. Twenty years had been sufficient to confirm that Spanish society was dynamic, modernising and innovative, in everything ranging from culture to the political structure of the State. The renewal that characterised everyday life also became a feature of politics.

As a political method, consensus has left the imprint of its advantages. In fact, it is protected by the Electoral Law itself. The law was drafted in order to avoid absolute majorities and to allow sub-national political parties to take part in national political life. Governments with absolute majorities were to be the exception and in my view it would be better for such exceptional circumstances, as occurred in 1982, not to happen again. Dialogue between parliamentary groups and long-standing pacts form part of our national political practice. Ignoring this new tradition of consensus can only lead to increasing tension and frustration which could either weaken leaders, forcing resignations at a faster rate than the parties can cope with or prevent other political options from emerging as a Centre party. Suárez's Democratic and Social Centre (CDS)[23] was the last major attempt by the Centrists and became a casualty of unpropitious times. If it had survived until today, it would have been able to play the role of a nationwide parliamentary alternative to the Left and Right in Spanish political life without excluding the nationalists. And had it been called upon to support a minority government, it would have been able to take the drama out of day to day politics, and to strengthen the mainstream consensus.

Suárez juggling with the UCD (its logo was created from the C and D of UCD). By Peridis.

Notes

1 Spain handed over its former colony to the joint custody of Morocco and Mauritania after the much-criticised Acuerdo de Madrid of 14 November 1975 during Franco's dying days.

2 The new King had kept the Francoist Prime Minister Carlos Arias Navarro in power.

3 As the overthrow of the Caetano dictatorship on 25 April 1974 was called.

4 Name given to politicians who favoured a limited opening up (*apertura*) of the dictatorial regime.

5 A view shared by many since a newspaper greeted the announcement with the headline *'¡Qué error, qué inmenso error!'* (What a terrible mistake!)

6   The Law provided for a bi-cameral parliament to reconvene after new elections and set out interim regulations for the electoral system. It made reference to popular sovereignty and provided elements for the rule of law, fundamental rights and a 'confused' cooperation/separation of powers. See San Román, P. (ed.), *El sistema político español*, Madrid: McGraw-Hill, p.24.

7 Tierno Galván was the veteran opposition leader of a group of socialists who formed the P. S. P. (Popular Socialist Party) which fused with the PSOE in 1978.

8 Perceived as an organ of censorship and control over the media.

9 It had won 29% of the vote in the June 1977 parliamentary elections, giving it 118 deputies to the government's 165.

10 Spain has had twelve constitutions since 1808.

11 Organic laws are the highest-ranking laws whose status is mid-way between the Constitution and ordinary laws (Newton & Donaghy, 1997: 63).

12 Apart from the División Azul sent to support the Nazis on the eastern front in World War II.

13 The veteran Communist poet Rafael Alberti even presided over the first post-electoral assembly of elected deputies, as the eldest of them all.

14 The coup attempt, led by Colonel Tejero of the Civil Guard and General Milans del Bosch, Captain-General of Valencia military region, failed after the King's forceful intervention persuaded the rest of the armed forces not to follow suit.

15 New Force, the far right political party which had won one seat in 1979.

16 The GRAPO ('popular revolutionary armed groups') was a shadowy far left group carrying out armed actions.

17 The Generalitat is the Catalan government. Led by Tarradellas, it remained in exile until it was resurrected in Barcelona and Tarradellas was able to return. He was succeeded by Jordi Pujol.

18 UGT: Unión General de Trabajadores (General Union of Workers); CO: Comisiones Obreras, Workers' Commissions, also a confederation.

19 Which is why Suárez did not take Spain into NATO. His successor, however, opted for entry via majority vote in parliament and did not hold a referendum.

20 The referendum, held in March 1986, proposed that Spain should remain in NATO on three conditions: that it would not integrate into NATO's military command structure, that Spain would remain a non-nuclear country and that the US's military presence would be progressively reduced.

21 MPAIC: Movimiento para la Autodeterminación y la Independencia del Archipiélago Canario, the Canary Island separatist group active at the time.

22 Important ETA members wanted by the Spanish police lived in France as political refugees since before the return to democracy and it took a long time for French procedures to change sufficiently to allow ETA members to be extradited as 'criminals'.

23 The Centro Democrático y Social was Suárez's attempt to relaunch his political career after resigning from UCD. It contested the elections of 1982, 1986 and 1989.

Translated by Kathryn Phillips-Miles and Monica Threlfall.
All footnotes by the editor.

4. Tackling the Economic Crisis: The government's consensual strategy

Juan Antonio García Díez (with J. Antonio Díaz López)

Juan Antonio García Díez was Minister for Economy and Trade during the second government of Adolfo Suárez. Born in Madrid in 1940, he graduated as an economist and became a specialist grade civil servant in 1966. A founder member of the Social Democrat Party that joined Suárez's Union of the Democratic Centre (UCD), he was elected to parliament in 1979 and became Minister for Economy and Trade in 1980. A friend of Leopoldo Calvo Sotelo, he remained in government after Suárez's resignation in January 1981 until the UCD lost the election the following year and he withdrew from politics. He is the author of The USSR 1917–23: From Revolution to Planning. *The last part of his career was in business, as Chairman of Uralita and Yamaha Motors España, amongst other positions. Juan Antonio García Díez died not long after writing this in 1998.*

Introduction

A quarter of a century has passed since Spain embarked on its transformation from a personalised dictatorship to a democratic system. Much has been published on the politics of this transition. Much less has been written about the economy or the hurdles that economic policy would come up against. This is the story that I will tell, drawing on my own personal experience as a member of the government from 1977–82.

I would like to begin by pointing out that difficulties that today seem so remote that they could hardly have existed were, at that time, of the utmost importance. The crucial task was to ensure a *peaceful* transition to a new political system. Let us not forget how quickly the factors that at the beginning of 1973 seemed to determine the outcome of the Franco period changed. The old regime envisaged a framework supported by two mainstays: a strong rhythm of economic growth and the appointment of a new Prime Minister (the first since the civil war) in June that year. Admiral Carrero Blanco was to be the guarantor of continuity. The framework crumbled within a few weeks. In October 1973, the first oil crisis destroyed the theory

41

of continued growth and Carrero Blanco was assassinated by ETA in December. A few months later, in April 1974, the Portuguese Revolution ended the long history of that other authoritarian regime of the Iberian Peninsula. Suddenly, everything had changed.

Some might say the transition can be dated back to then. In order to attempt to understand the economic history – as opposed to just the economy – of this period, it might be useful to briefly refer to the three principal themes which, in my opinion, provided the structure of the process: crisis, change and learning.

Crisis

There was a crisis in the world economy. The rapid growth in the economies of the First World that had prevailed since the beginning of the post World War recovery took an abrupt nose-dive with the first oil crisis, and continued to fall with the second. A period of slow growth began, domestic and foreign balances became more difficult to maintain and public expenditure became noticeably weaker. Being a country with no energy sources of its own, Spain was most vulnerable to this crisis. In addition, the crisis was not tackled effectively between 1973–5. As a result, during the transition, our economy had to absorb the effects of the two oil price hikes almost simultaneously.

This coincided with a crisis in economic ideas, both in the theory of how to manage advanced industrial economies and in the underlying ideology. It was the beginning of the process which would take us from Keynesianism to out-and-out deregulation and, on a purely ideological level, to the crisis in social democracy and to the revival of liberalism following the waning of authoritarian socialism.

Change

Change had taken place prior to the crisis yet the crisis required more of it. Spain had already undergone a social transformation during its development years. A poor country had become modestly comfortable, in the process leaving behind a basically rural, hierarchical and deeply religious society for an urban, liberal and secular one. The transformation made political change both possible and necessary.

Democratisation altered the way the economy worked because new economic actors were able to have their say, unbalancing the previous status quo. In particular, the new situation released demands that had previously had no outlet for expression: society as a whole was demanding more public services and a more developed welfare state; trade unions, now free, were demanding higher wages; the regional political entities, the Autonomous Communities, were coming into being and the newly elected town councils were demanding greater authority and more resources; the State was looking to raise more taxes and more sources of revenue to make up for the inadequate base which would in turn lead to higher interest rates.

Learning

Spaniards would have the none-too-easy task of learning to live with freedom. The business world had to learn to deal with the new self-governing institutions, trade unions, business organisations and lobbies, and regional and local government. Spaniards had to abandon ideological stereotypes beloved of the last isolated years of the Franco period. Old socialists were learning to evolve into social-democrats and the right-wing interventionism of the Francoists was giving way to liberalism. All had to learn the new rules of joint decision-making, and respect for the constraints imposed by pluralism and having to deal with many social agents.

These three themes recur in the course of this account. We will begin by explaining our starting-point, then examine how economic policy was conducted during the period after 1973, which could be called the pre-transition. Then we will review the main courses of action of the UCD governments in order to examine the philosophy underlying these actions and the limitations placed on them by the behaviour of social and political agents.

1. The Starting Point

In 1973, Spain's GDP rose to the enviable real growth rate of 8.1 per cent, with full employment: unemployment was 1.2 per cent! For the third year in a row, the balance of payments on the current account reflected what was for the time a significant surplus (more than 500 million dollars). The only blot on this brilliant landscape was the increasing rate of inflation. The increase in the RPI had jumped to an annualised average rate of 11.5 per cent compared with 8.3 per cent in 1972.

Of course, everything was not a bed of roses. We were living through 'the autumn of the patriarch'[1] and the impending 'fulfilment of the provisions for the succession', as the post-Franco future was called. Both introduced a substantial element of uncertainty with regard to the country's future political development. The dictatorship had become more moderate and no longer seemed to have sufficient strength to ensure its survival intact. Neither was it capable of completely dominating Spanish society, in spite of isolated acts of repression, as workers fought for and gained higher wages.

Rapid economic growth had concealed weaknesses in the Spanish economy which now became apparent. Economic recovery had led to such a high degree of complacency about what had been achieved – not confined to government circles – that essential facts were overlooked. Firstly, that in spite of the country's rapid modernisation, the structure of the business sector was still found wanting. This could be seen in the size of companies, even the largest of which were comparatively small; in their poor financial structures which made them very sensitive to variations in costs and to the availability of credit; and in their low technological endowments and old-fashioned management structures – the former a result of the limited capacity to produce home-grown technology and the latter caused by short-sightedness on the part of the business class itself.

Secondly, it was often forgotten that our economic growth had not created much new employment. In 1974, the working population reached a peak in Spanish history: nearly 13 million, having increased in the ten years since 1964 by a little more than a million. Engaged in the process of destroying numerous agricultural jobs while gaining large increases in industrial productivity, the Spanish economy usually only created 100,000 new jobs a year. Equilibrium in the labour market – a labour market in which, for demographic and social reasons, a low proportion of the population participated –

was achieved thanks to a flow of emigrants which almost matched that of job-creation in size.

Thirdly, the economy worked with a particular structure of relative prices which would soon be adversely affected by the imminent oil crisis, by increasing wage claims and by the need to raise the real cost of borrowing.

Finally, a factor which partly explains the persistence of the traits already discussed: a web of interventionist practices and institutional inflexibility on the part of the state severely restricted the economy's ability to adapt to new circumstances and effectively to reassign the available resources. This inflexibility was in the nature of the dictatorship, but by the end it was less a matter of fixed ideas than of bureaucratic privileges and interests. A study of the inflexibility of state structures inherited from the Franco years requires more space than we can give it here, but the following areas can be highlighted.

- Industrial relations had been subjected to a 'social pact' by the previous regime which meant no freedom to strike or join a trade union and, in return, growing social security provision and severe restrictions on employers making workers redundant or moving them around.
- The public sector was small and supported by an insufficient and inefficient tax system which nevertheless managed to be omnipresent as an interventionist and regulatory authority.
- The foreign sector, the liberalisation of which had begun in 1959 and was abruptly stopped in 1964 without gaining any further stimulus than that derived from the strongly criticised but brilliant preferential trade agreement with the EEC in 1970, maintained restrictions on imports, distrusted foreign investment, and kept up exchange-rate controls dating back to 1939.
- The financial system was plagued by entrenched privileges, restricted access to a series of closed financial networks, and the maintenance of very low returns on savings, in real terms.

These would be the major areas in urgent need of reform once it was plain that our economy had to adapt to the new circumstances created by Franco's death and the lingering effects of the oil crisis. Also in need of reform were our productive sectors themselves. Our agricultural policy was a mixture of an absurd caricature of the EEC's Common Agricultural Policy and the remnants of old Falangist ideas from Castile and Andalusia. Our industry closely reflected the situation we have just described: protected from foreign competition, overmanned and, in many cases, dependent on privileged financing. It is not surprising that the need to implement a serious restructuring was identified at the earliest stages of the transition.

In October 1973 came the first oil price hike of 60 per cent that would shake Spain out of its complacency. Although they did not directly affect Spain, the embargo measures put into place plunged Western Europe into a mood of pessimism and concern, which was accentuated by further price rises. By the beginning of 1974, the price of a barrel of light crude was around nine dollars (F.O.B. before shipping from the Persian Gulf), some four times greater than the 2.32 dollars it had cost in August 1973.

2. The Pre-transition

The governments in power before democracy was established in 1977 had, therefore, to deal with a serious economic shock, under conditions of increasing political uncertainty. In its report for 1973 the Bank of Spain estimated that the impact of the oil crisis on the Spanish economy would be around three per cent of GDP. These three percentage points would be taken away from domestic demand and would be transferred to the producer-countries by means of a substantial deterioration in the balance of payments on the current account. And the mechanism for taking them away would inevitably be a rise in prices or a reduction in tax income. Inflationary pressures added to an already complicated situation, as price increases had been the main black mark against the Spanish economy. As a result wages also rose by 19.8 per cent per hour in one year alone, helped by full employment and a super-expansive monetary policy. For example liquidity had grown by an average approaching 24 per cent per annum.

Seen in retrospect, the surprising reaction to the crisis gave rise to problems which could have had serious consequences for the introduction of a democratic system. Distancing themselves from what would be the more orthodox reaction of other Western countries faced with the crisis, the Spanish government decided to tackle it by 'compensating' for it.

The compensatory policy was based on a rather unclear hypothesis about the performance of the international economy: the imminent recession in the West would be short-lived because the OPEC cartel would break up and oil prices would go down again, or because the Western countries understood that restrictive policies would not solve the problem. Spain, which was starting from a good position on its balance of payments, need not shy away from growth. It could, so to speak, surf over the recession and meet up again with the Western economies in the ascendant stage of the next cycle. Furthermore, both to physically guarantee our oil supply and to be in an advantageous position, we had the trump card of our traditional friendship with the Arab world.

Based on this reasoning, which the facts showed to be completely nonsensical, a policy was put in place. A whole series of fiscal measures were taken, the expansionary effect of which was estimated at two per cent of GDP. Economic growth would be in excess of five per cent. Increases in the money supply of up to 20 per cent would be accepted. The resulting substantial deficit would be easy to finance with reserves and loans. This was the policy put in place for 1974.

We were already in crisis. But economic growth within the OECD was practically nil in 1974 and seemed as if it would even be negative in 1975. In October 1974, there was a cabinet reshuffle and responsibility for economic policy was placed in more orthodox hands. Unfortunately, the orthodoxy could not impose its criteria for long enough in a political and social situation that was rapidly deteriorating towards the truly surrealist autumn of Franco's death. In a further U-turn, the new people in charge of economic policy from the beginning of 1976 again kissed goodbye to prudence and launched the economy on the path of expansion, combining a devaluation of the peseta in February 1976 with an upwards revision of the objectives of monetary policy which would remove the last brakes on prices and salaries. In the month of May alone, prices rose in excess of 4 per cent – one more nail in the coffin of the King's first government. The period from May until an elected government took over in July 1977 was one of 'just getting by'. But political reform took precedence over tackling the imbalances of a deteriorating economy in serious need of adjustment.

3. Restructuring and Reform

The outlook for the new government in the summer of 1977 was unpromising. On the one hand, the economy was afflicted with serious structural problems, some of which were almost endemic, and others which were clearly the product of rapid development from 1960–74. On the other hand, there were grave problems of an immediate nature that had arisen as a result of the way in which the oil crisis had been tackled. It was faced with the legacy of three and a half years of a mistaken economic policy. By mid-1977 consumer prices were increasing at an annual rate of 38 per cent and wages by 24 per cent. Looking back, I now cannot help thinking 'you must have been joking' when the incoming PSOE government complained about the difficult situation it had inherited. It was the UCD, not the PSOE, who had had to deal with the effects of the irresponsible reactions to the crisis. These ranged from denial ('no problem here') in 1974–5, and resignation ('there is nothing to be done') in 1976–7, to the workers' opportunism ('our time has come') and the capitalists' flightiness ('let's get out of here').

Following the Moncloa Pacts, signed on 25 October 1977, economic policy would evolve along two central axes, each of which had an influence on the other. These were known respectively as 'restructuring' and 'reform'. Restructuring was concerned with the short term and with the prevailing conjuncture. It sought to re-establish equilibrium in the balance of payments and in prices. It began with a significant devaluation as soon as the government was formed, continued with a tighter monetary policy and was wrapped up with a pact agreeing to control the rise of pay settlements.

What was labelled 'reform' was more concerned with the long term and attempted to deal with the structural problems in the economy. While it was accepted that the economy had to function with a greater degree of freedom, public spending was to increase at the same time, both as a matter of principle and because it was the counterpart of the sacrifice of the workers in agreeing to lower wage demands. As a corollary of increased public spending, fiscal reform to augment state revenues was envisaged, also a part of the compensation package to the workers. This Moncloa Pact plan was implemented, with slight nuances, during the entire period the UCD was in power. It combined generally strict monetary policy with the continuous use of an incomes policy, growth of public spending and a higher tax burden, all accompanied by structural reforms intended to be generally liberalising.

Initially, the restructuring programme was very successful. Perhaps it could have been bolder, but it did de-politicise economic problems during the period when the

Constitution was being drafted and helped imbalances to be substantially reduced by the beginning of 1979. The balance of payments on the current account went into surplus and the Spanish inflation differential with respect to other OECD countries was reduced from 15 to 6 percentage points.

The economy was therefore in a position to start growing again when, shortly after the general election of 1979 which confirmed the UCD in government, the second oil crisis began. This became more and more serious until the price of a barrel of crude oil reached its highest level of 37 dollars in 1981. The government's reaction now was far swifter than it had been during the first crisis, but nothing could prevent the end of falling inflation, or the economy from becoming almost stagnant, or the balance of payments from suddenly worsening. The deterioration became acute because of the initial decision to keep the peseta relatively high which led to a brief government crisis in the spring of 1980.

Under these circumstances, the incomes policy continued to be extensively applied throughout the entire period in varying forms, from statutory enforcement by means of a decree-law, to union-employer pacts, to tripartite agreements with the government. There is little doubt that during this entire period the policy was useful both as an anti-inflationary weapon and as a means of maintaining social peace. It also had its negative side, however, pushing up public spending and restricting the depth of some reforms which were not to the liking of the workers and the parties of the Left. The incomes policy was therefore the balancing factor in the tension between a generally expansive fiscal policy and a mostly contractive monetary policy.

The fiscal reform was successful but a high political price was ultimately paid. A modern and reasonably progressive tax system was established, in agreement with the Left, together with a very generous tax amnesty. Despite technical imperfections, it was effective in introducing progressivity into the Spanish tax system without unduly disturbing public opinion not only throughout the UCD period, but during the PSOE era as well. But it proved to be almost unacceptable to the right-wing businessmen and was one of the seeds of the subsequent confrontation between the UCD and the CEOE – the Spanish confederation of business organisations – who called the ministers in charge 'crypto-socialists'. It was only once the effective marginal rate of personal income tax went up from 40 per cent to 56 per cent during the socialist period that people began to think that Enrique Fuentes Quintana's and Francisco Fernández Ordóñez's earlier reforms had not been so bad after all.

In contrast, the industrial relations reform which led to the 1980 Workers' Statute, was a lost opportunity to change radically the inflexibility inherited from the Francoist system. The fundamental problem was that it still protected employees to such a high degree that any reduction in the size of the payroll through redundancies was still an extraordinarily difficult and costly exercise. There were obviously political reasons behind this, but out of all the UCD government's actions this was probably one of the few that later proved to be detrimental to the economy.

The introduction of the new system of financing the regional governments was more difficult to put into effect and its consequences were harder to foresee. Today it is widely believed that the system established in the law financing the Autonomous

Communities, known as LOFCA[2], was essentially ineffective, unstable and costly. It certainly provided future policy-makers with a complex inheritance, but at that time it was much more difficult to predict what problems it might lead to.

It was also during this period that unemployment, the most serious problem afflicting the Spanish economy even today, began to raise its head. Firstly, the traditional escape valve of emigration had ceased to function. On the contrary, significant numbers of workers who had lost their jobs in other European countries were returning to Spain. To make matters worse, the slow growth in the economy – due to the stabilisation policy which was necessary to offset the effects of two oil crises – not only did not create jobs, it actually destroyed them. Lastly, a problem common to all developed economies, namely the weakness of investment, had become exacerbated in Spain due to psychological and political as well as economic reasons. Business was in the process of adapting to the new situation, radically different from the past, and felt disorientated, even discouraged. On top of that, the labour legislation forced them to spend some of their investment resources on very costly staff reductions.

Therefore the economy grew very little while the UCD was in power, although not much less than in the other European economies, and unemployment increased significantly. Public spending and the budget deficit increased substantially, although public debt was kept at very moderate levels. And while significant progress was made in reforming the economy, it was too gradual. Nonetheless, these problems never became an obstacle in the process of establishing and consolidating a democratic system.

4. The UCD's Economic Ideas

The reasons behind the UCD government's choice of economic policy were political, theoretical and practical. In fact, the first democratic government came to power convinced that economic policy had to be, somewhat paradoxically, both more liberal and more social-democratic in nature. The government thought it was necessary to reduce the hitherto interventionist role played by the omnipresent Francoist public sector but also believed that the role of the state as the provider of certain services, especially public services, had to be increased. The economic programme used by the UCD to fight the 1977 general election reflected this, and it became probably the best kept election promise in the history of our, admittedly brief, democracy. The UCD put in place a programme to deregulate the economy and deliberately raise public spending with the help of higher and progressive taxation. One should remember the UCD came to power at a time when the social-democratic model of paying for a welfare state through taxes was not in dispute. In addition, they faced a PSOE whose economic thinking was still Keynesian. UCD also believed in a considerable amount of anti-interventionist liberalism, which was particularly appropriate after a dictatorship that had been decidedly over-regulatory in its zeal to control society.

Apart from these political reasons for its policy orientation, the UCD also followed the economic theory that appropriate use of monetary instruments would make it possible to determine the pace of GDP growth in nominal terms – this even came up occasionally in ministers' speeches. The forecasts for the budget deficit and the balance of payments were elements to be introduced in a monetary budget which would theoretically result in growth, in nominal terms, of the economy. The way in which this nominal growth would be allocated between prices and real growth would then be determined by the social partners, the two sides of industry, in their wage negotiations. This explains the importance placed on the incomes policy throughout the entire period. A final reason why UCD made their choices was a practical one. Of all possible economic policy instruments, none is more advanced in its design nor has such a safe statistical basis as monetary control. The techniques designed by the Bank of Spain since the beginning of the 1970s were among the best applied by Western central banks. They involved accepting the free fluctuation of interest rates and, to a certain extent, of exchange rates too. Of course, this monetary policy later ran into many problems, aggravated by the effects of Spain having a more open economy.

5. Political and Social Actors

Another factor to consider is how economic policy during the transition had to be highly context-sensitive, given the attitudes of the new political actors, the reactions of business leaders and the complex nature of the governing party itself.

The influence of the conservative Popular Alliance, the Communist Party (PCE), the regional and the nationalist parties on economic policy was generally limited to their involvement in particular matters or to exchanging specific parliamentary support for certain concessions. As the largest opposition group, the PSOE had more weight, despite the fact that it was going through its own internal process of change and learning experiences. One could say that the UCD is to be thanked for managing to stop the socialists from gaining power until their own 'transition' had been at least partially completed. For when one re-reads the resolutions of the PSOE's 27th Congress of December 1976, just a few months before the first election, they seem to belong to another country and another party. Reaffirming its marxist analysis, the PSOE addressed itself to an 'anti-capitalist bloc of classes'. It intended moving to a socialist economy with the goal of replacing 'capitalist businesses with self-managed businesses'. Once democracy was stable, the PSOE proposed reforms involving 'a programme of nationalisations, a substantial change in the current power structure of large companies, both industrial and agricultural, and a planning process to ensure the co-ordination of the economy in the public interest'.

Fortunately, none of this was too serious, as borne out by later events, but at the time the PSOE was full of leftist prejudices over economic policy, and their evolution was slow. In parliamentary budget debates the PSOE would often support public spending increases, arguing that there was no need to get obsessed with the public debt issue. Innumerable cases went on record where their position was the complete opposite of what they defended once in power. Their change of heart can be put down to several factors, namely: the growing maturity of the PSOE leadership; the lessons learned from the unorthodox experience of French socialism during its two first years of government in 1981–3; the fact that the priority issues demanding attention in the areas of fiscal policy and the welfare state had already been dealt with by the UCD governments; and, finally, the individual personalities and political beliefs of the socialist finance ministers. However transformed and groomed for the task the PSOE seemed by 1982, their earlier strange behaviour in opposition very often complicated the implementation of UCD economic policy between 1977–82.

Regarding the social partners, the irony was that for most of the 1977–82 period, the government's relationship with the trade unions was generally better than with the organisations representing business – and that this turned out to be the mirror image of what would happen later on to the socialist governments. As mentioned earlier, one of the biggest economic problems the UCD faced was the fall in investment – gross investment in capital assets fell from 25 per cent of GDP in 1974 to only 20 per cent in 1982 (and continued the downward trend until 1985). There were strictly economic reasons for this, such as the rise in oil prices, the severe inroads made into company profits, and companies' difficulties in raising capital from external sources. While these reasons were objective, there were other reasons accounting for limited investment which were less so. Spanish employers, along with those of the rest of Europe were engulfed by a wave of pessimism regarding the prospects for capitalism. And in addition, now that strikes had become legal in Spain, business felt frightened by the newly emboldened behaviour of the workers and tended to interpret purely economic demands as if they were political problems.

Unlike the trade unions, the employers' confederation (CEOE) did not take part in the Moncloa Pacts, and followed a very political agenda from the beginning. Rather than staying outside party-politics, they expressed their dissatisfaction with the 'social-democratic' policies of the UCD governments and supported Fraga's line that there must be a 'natural majority' for the right in Spain – clearly a mistaken diagnosis at that point in its history. This politicisation culminated in the Andalusian Employers' Confederation joining in the campaign against the PSOE in the regional elections of May 1982. Not surprisingly, when a business community which is already burdened with real problems constantly receives from its leaders the message that a nominally centre-right government is governing against its interests and making a mess of things, it is disinclined to invest. It is a story that has hardly been studied but which goes a long way towards explaining the Spanish economy's poor performance. Only in 1985, with a world-wide boom underway and after it had become convinced that the PSOE no longer represented a danger to the capitalist system, did the business community begin to make serious investments.

The third non-economic factor to bear in mind is the situation of the UCD itself. By 1979 the Party, to its credit, had made an outstanding success of the constitutional process and significant progress in streamlining the economy. But that year the first democratic local government elections were held, which resulted in the post of mayor being taken by a post-electoral coalition of socialists and communists in many cities[3]. From that point onwards, UCD came under heightened external pressure from the nationalist parties (aware of their potential for parliamentary bargaining), from the PSOE (who played a two-handed opposition game, now responsible and judicious, now ultra-critical), and from the Popular Alliance Party and the CEOE (claiming their 'natural majority'). Such pressures threatened to break up the alliance which had created the UCD in 1977. The problem for UCD was not that there was too much ideological dispute, as people believed at the time, but that there were too many leaders and aspiring leaders. 1980 was a year of decline, marked by the government's failure to win an endorsement of its autonomy policy in the referendum for the Andalusian region – a setback that was unlikely to encourage new investment. 1981 could hardly have been worse, with Suárez resigning on 29 January, and the rightist military coup attempt on 23 February. The full parliament was taken hostage during the ceremony to invest the new Prime Minister, and held for 24 hours.

In the first months of 1981, Suárez's successor Leopoldo Calvo-Sotelo enjoyed what could be called a 'window of opportunity'. He could have formed a grand coalition government of Right and Left to isolate the plotters and their sympathisers, or called a general election to set Spanish politics on a new course. Instead, he merely reshuffled the UCD government and concentrated on four questions: bringing the coup plotters to justice, reaching a pact on the autonomy process, making a social pact, and taking Spain into NATO. These were all scrupulously carried out but left no energy for thinking about nor for acting on what would come later. The constant deterioration of the international economy swept our own along with it. Together with the increasing arrogance of their opponents, it accelerated the break up of the UCD as a party. After the Galician autonomy elections in October 1981 and after Fernández Ordóñez's group had left the Party that same autumn, there was still an opportunity before the Andalusian regional elections of May 1982 to win sufficient popular backing to ensure the survival of what was left of the UCD. But UCD lost the election, and by the time Suárez left the Party on 31 July 1982 to form his own group, the Democratic and Social Centre (CDS), it was clear that the end had come: the government would have insufficient support for parliament to approve the budget for 1982 without which its hands would be tied.

Without the government's ability to implement tough policies, the economy suffered. Calvo Sotelo, the Prime Minister, felt obliged to call an early general election for October 1982. Yet, despite adverse circumstances, the economy was handed over in fairly reasonable shape to the new government in December of that year. Arguably, the economy was in much better shape than the figures later reflected. Of course, 1982 was the worst for the Western world since the completion of the post-war reconstruction and particularly bad for Spain. Nonetheless, the current deficit in the balance of payments had improved over 1981 and at 2.4 per cent of GDP was below the 1976 record and below the figure it would reach ten years later. Our inflationary differential with regard to the EC (using the private consumption deflator) was 4.3 percentage points and this would not significantly improve until 1985. The new government cleverly shifted the blame onto its predecessors, increasing prices in December that in the normal course of events would not have risen until 1983, and altering the accounting criteria used for income and public expenditure in order to increase the budget deficit for 1982. Even the Bank of Spain, which was generally respectful of the government of the day, recognised in its Annual Report for 1982 (page 61) and in its Economic Bulletin (January 1983) that between 200,000 million and 300,000 million pesetas of the deficit had been transferred from 1983 to the previous year.

Conclusion

If I had to sum up in a nutshell, I would describe the period as revolutionary in the most profound sense of the word – the first victorious and peaceful revolution in Spain's history. The rules of the political game had been radically changed; new social and economic actors, silent for four decades, had found an increasingly prominent voice. Of course, the economy could not but be affected by this far-reaching change. Economic policy had to deal with short-term adjustments and launch structural reforms, trying to ensure that economic problems did not put the political process in danger. With hindsight I believe that this fundamental priority was more than satisfactorily achieved. True, the economy did not grow much and the progress made in many areas is now considered to have been too gradual. But if one considers the economic impact of other processes of political change, one has to accept that the positive aspects outweigh the negative ones.

After the PSOE's triumph in the general election in 1982, a particular interpretation of Spain's recent economic history was popularised and gained currency. It went as follows: after a remarkably cohesive effort by the chief political actors to forestall the economic crisis, exemplified by the Moncloa Pacts, the UCD government became increasingly more right-wing and weak, so that scant attention was paid to economic problems because there was greater interest in politics, and that all this led to the unsustainable situation towards the end of 1982. But in fact, the economy that the UCD handed over to its successors was stronger than thought at the time. For a start, they inherited an economic policy blueprint both for the short-term and for longer-term reform which would continue to be applied to a large extent. Socialist economic policy was, paradoxically, to have much more in common with the UCD's first electoral programme than with the conclusions reached at the PSOE's Twenty-Seventh Congress of December 1976.

To return to something we have already highlighted throughout, the Spanish economy still faces many problems and weaknesses. And in retrospect, all that was achieved in the late 1970s and 1980s now looks easy and not radical enough. But on 20 November 1975, no one would have imagined that Spain would have developed as much as it has in only two decades.

Notes

1   A reference to the title of García Márquez's novel *El Otoño del Patriarca*.
2   LOFCA: Ley Orgánica de Financiación de las Comunidades Autónomas.
3   An amendment introduced during the parliamentary debate on the municipal bill meant that the mayor was not elected on a plurality of the votes but needed to form a majority alliance, mirroring the national system.

Translation By Kathryn Phillips-Miles and Monica Threlfall.
All footnotes by the editor.

5. The Consensus-building Role of the Spanish Communist Party

Santiago Carrillo

Santiago Carrillo was General Secretary of the Communist Party of Spain (PCE) from 1960–82. Born in 1915, at 19 he became leader of the youth wing of the Socialist Party (PSOE), and headed its fusion with the Communist Youth Organisation. The Unified Socialist Youth (JSU) is credited with playing an important role in the 1936 defence of Madrid. Carrillo joined the Communist Party in the autumn of that year and spent most of the rest of the civil war in Catalonia until it fell to the Nationals in 1938. During Carrillo's leadership, the PCE in exile distanced itself from the USSR and was critical of the 1968 Soviet invasion of Czechoslovakia. He became an exponent of 'eurocommunism', the European parliamentary road to socialism. After returning secretly to Madrid in 1976, Carrillo became one of the main protagonists of the transition to democracy and was a deputy for Madrid from 1977. He resigned as General Secretary in November 1982 after the PCE obtained less than four per cent of the vote and lost 19 of its 23 seats. He is the author of numerous books including the well-known Eurocommunism and the State.

I was a member of the leadership of the Communist Party of Spain (PCE) for forty-eight years, from 1937–85, and held the position of General Secretary for twenty-two years. I was expelled in 1985 together with about twenty other members of the Party's Central Committee and its Executive. Several thousand members and cadres also left the Party in a gesture of solidarity.

I will disappoint anyone who expects me to do what so many who are no longer in the PCE have done, namely to condemn communist ideas, practices and people and to say that communism is an abomination. I still feel that I am a communist and I do not disown my personal history. For many years, the Communist Party was the party that made the most sacrifices for the sake of democracy in Spain. I have met the most honest and generous people in its ranks, who would lay down their lives for the good of others.

It is impossible to discuss the Spanish communists' politics during the transition without referring to one fundamental piece of background history. In 1956, the PCE worked out what we called our national reconciliation policy. Little did we know that

From devil to statesman in a few steps:
Santiago Carillo's first television appearance, May 1977. By Peridis.

is was to inspire the transition to democracy twenty years later. At that time, no other party thought in this way, and the victors' side[1] even less so. Already at that time, we were suggesting the idea of reconciliation based on democratic freedom for everyone, on an amnesty that would cancel out the responsibility for accusations of crimes directed at both sides, and on moving beyond the politics of revenge that still hovered in the air. Our intention was to put the full and final stop to the lingering war and extinguish any spark that might set it alight once more. This background will explain why the PCE, in its conduct during the transition, gave consummate proof of its commitment to democratisation and of its feeling of responsibility for the general interests of the country.

One of the problems we confronted which most clearly put our sense of responsibility to the test was how to define the form of the new Spanish state. The PCE had defended the Republic right up to its last hours before defeat in 1939.[2] It had taken up arms to confront the coalition formed in Madrid from sections of the PSOE, anarcho-syndicalists and other Republicans to launch a coup d'état against Negrín's government, a coup which ended up surrendering to Franco.[3] The PCE was the party of Republican resistance to the death. With this background, it would be very difficult, years later, to accept a monarchy with a king appointed by Franco.

In politics, however, one must learn to measure realistically the strength of the forces one is up against. The democratic opposition knew that they were not powerful enough to achieve a change in the regime on their own. They had tried unsuccessfully to find allies within the army, and even in Don Juan de Borbón[4], who would be capable of moving a section of the regime's forces towards the opposition's position. All in vain.

Then suddenly, with Adolfo Suárez's appointment, the regime insiders who were closet reformists came out into the open. Now who was the political leader of these reformers? Who had surreptitiously gathered some of them together, waiting for the time when Franco would no longer be in control? No less a person than Juan Carlos himself! He was prepared to introduce democracy if it allowed him to keep his crown. All this became abundantly clear to me, basically as a result of two conversations I had with Don José María de Areilza[5] and because I had closely watched events. This is not to say that Suárez's personal style and courage did anything but greatly accelerate the speed with which Gordian knots were cut or difficult obstacles were swept aside during the transition. However, before coming to government, Adolfo Suárez had been a civil servant without the pulling-power to achieve what was called 'The Reform' on his own. The real political leader of the regime reformists, at least until 1978 when the Constitution was approved, was the King.

Stated in this way, it is clear that there would only be agreement between the regime and the opposition if the latter accepted the monarchy.[6] For even if the Left had had the power to impose a referendum before the constituent period, which it did not have, the monarchical solution would still have been chosen and would have constituted the approved form of the State. However, this would have meant that the form of the State would have emerged from a referendum *defeat* of the Left – a dangerous question. For in a country where the differences between the Left and Right had caused a civil war and a dictatorship for almost forty years, the new monarchy would have been perceived as having been imposed by the Right. Even more seriously, the Constitution of 1978, drawn up in the midst of this struggle, might have ended up being less democratic. The Right would have tried to draft a document giving the monarchy much more power and making it less subject to parliament.[7]

I am not talking through my hat here, because during the time the Constitution was being drawn up, there were proposals to this effect which were only withdrawn because of the concerns expressed – not least by convinced monarchists themselves – that the monarchy should be re-established with the agreement of all political forces. Perhaps because of this, it is not incorrect to describe our monarchy as very similar to a democratic republic. The underlying problems of the Spanish monarchy are no different from those of European republics. We are governed by parliamentary majorities in any case.

I therefore believe that the Left was politically astute in accepting the monarchic form of the state. If any other form had been approved, there would have been no agreement between the reformers of the regime and the opposition and we would have experienced substitute, hybrid, forms of Francoism that might have been able to postpone the re-establishment of our democratic freedoms for a long time. Furthermore, we would not have been able to defeat the coup d'état on 23 February 1981 without the King's forceful intervention.

I would argue that the PCE's attitude at that time was decisive in determining the stance taken by the Left. If the PCE had not shown firm judgement and avoided demagogic rhetoric, it is doubtful whether the Left as a whole would have adopted the intelligent position that it did.

Another significant event during the transition were the talks that culminated in the Moncloa Pacts, a set of agreements reached in September 1977 by Suárez with the leaders of the newly elected parliamentary parties and the trade union confederations. Most commentators generally only refer to their economic clauses and forget all about their political and social contents. It was the latter which contained the fundamentals, the heart of the Pacts, which is not to deny the importance of the economic side as well. They help to explain one significant fact about the negotiation of the Moncloa Pacts: the conservative leader of the Alianza Popular[8], Manuel Fraga, only signed the economic agreements and refused to sign the political ones, that is, those concerning the 'Partial and Urgent Reforms to Adapt Legislation to the Appropriate Demands of the New Democratic Reality'. This section included measures to guarantee freedom of expression, freedom to attend meetings and take part in protests, and to join political parties, as well as individual freedoms such as the decriminalisation of adultery, of keeping a mistress, of the use of contraceptives – so representative of our backwardness at that time. There were also important measures such as the abolition of the so-called offences against Franco's Fundamental Laws[9], a revised concept of public order and the role of the police forces.

The social section included a series of clearly progressive measures, as follows: to increase the number of unemployed people receiving benefits; to move towards progressive taxation; to increase the total wages bill by 22 per cent with a more favourable deal for the lowest paid; to democratise the educational system; to create 400,000 primary school places, 200,000 nursery school places and 100,000 secondary school places; to give teachers better pay – in brief, a catalogue of gains for the Left. Apart from developing social policy in a positive way, there was a series of measures intended to reduce inflation and restructure the economy.

Beyond their actual contents, the Moncloa Pacts were valuable in one further crucial respect: they constituted the first written document in which agreement between the opposition and the reformers of the regime was firmly registered, rather than one side acquiescing or grudgingly accepting what the other had done. Most notably, this document was written and signed after the Communists had spent months developing the political strategy that it ultimately contained.

It is not often that pacts begin to be implemented before they have even been written; this, however, was one of the characteristics of the Spanish transition. And if political agreements are usually made between allied parties who may even have collaborated previously, in the Spanish case, the agreements were made between sides who had previously been overtly antagonistic to each other. Here the victors and the vanquished of yesteryear were collaborating closely, imbuing the Moncloa Pacts with a deep symbolism – of enemies finally burying the hatchet.

Needless to say, the talks started in an atmosphere of mistrust on both sides. What did each one propose to do? At the beginning, Suárez seemed to head a bloc of Francoists at varying stages of evolution. He could not sign such an agreement without coming into conflict with most of this block, beginning with the chiefs of the armed forces. The points of agreement came out in private conversations between individuals from both sides, in such a way that they could remain hidden or even be easily denied. This form of back and forth informal dialogue helped to build confidence about the aims of the meeting and in the sincerity of the negotiators. Actually it was only after Suárez had become leader of his own party, the UCD, and had won a democratic election, that he had the room for manoeuvre and could enter into a precise agreement.[10] Only then was he able to ignore the reluctance of the Francoists who had accompanied him during the reform process of 1976 but were ultimately disappointed by the subsequent course of events.

It was not easy to reach the final agreement of the Moncloa Pacts. Alianza Popular was against them and, as I have already mentioned, Fraga represented the Party at the meetings but did not sign the political section in the Pacts in which the development of democracy was envisaged. Neither were the socialists (PSOE) very enthusiastic about the Pacts. They would have preferred to have had an exclusive bilateral agreement with the UCD and to ignore the other parties, particularly the PCE. An exclusive agreement with the UCD would have strengthened the two-party politics favoured by the PSOE. At the time, they still had not discounted the possibility that the Italian political model might be reproduced in Spain, with a strong Communist Party widely represented in the institutions.

Much has been made of the Communists' *moderation* during the transition. However, little value or even attention has been given to the biggest concession that we, the Communists, made during that process. This concession seriously constrained the success of the PCE's parliamentary representation, reduced to twenty members in the first parliament,[11] despite the fact that our role during the resistance to Franco had been so significant that it had led to widespread predictions of far better results. I am referring here to the statement made by the Army High Command condemning the lifting of the ban on the Communist Party that Easter Saturday (9 April 1977) and also to the ensuing political commotion,[12] which was enough to cause many people to fear that peaceful change would be interrupted and that the planned elections might not be held. The statement carried an unabashed threat of a new *coup d'état* and an imperative message from the army to the electorate for the forthcoming elections: 'Beware of voting for the PCE!'. The army's interference in domestic politics was tantamount to a violation of the free vote, and was an attempt to maintain their veto against the Communist Party. These were the very generals who had waged war with Franco and upheld a terrorist dictatorship for forty years. If the government had had the power to do so at that time, the logical thing would have been to sack the High Command. But, at that time, the army had more power than the government and could have removed it and re-established a military regime. The government was forced to bite its tongue and put up with the military's rebuke.[13]

At that moment, the PCE held the fate of the transition in its hands. If, instead of accepting the Spanish flag, our Central Committee had published a statement[14] declaring that the stance taken by the army leaders did not allow Spaniards to vote freely, that the elections were discredited, given the lack of freedom of choice, and that the Communists refused to take part in them, what would have happened? If we had replied in this way, rising to the challenge thrown down by the generals, just as some of them probably thought we would, it is very likely that Suárez and the ministers most resolutely in favour of democratisation would have had to resign. At that moment the PCE irrefutably demonstrated its great sense of responsibility.

It should not be forgotten that only four or five members of the government personally backed the legalisation of the Communist Party for the first elections. The rest were taken by surprise and either resigned or accepted what was by then a done deal. Therefore our response was helpful to Suárez. We not only recognised the favour he had done us by taking the risk in legalising the PCE. Our stance really allowed the process of democratisation to move ahead, and even though the conditions for the elections were discriminatory towards the Communists[15], holding an election was crucial to freedom and democracy in Spain. We realised we needed to move on to the new stage as soon as possible and so we skirted around the objections raised by the old Francoist generals.

The PCE was inspired by a sincere and determined desire for democracy, developed during a long period of anti-fascist struggle that had taught us to value freedom greatly. As a result of an internal ideological debate in the PCE in the 1960s[16], the Spanish communist leaders had even adopted a critical stance towards Lenin's position on democracy. Against Lenin, we believed that democracy had existed before the state. Forms of democracy had already existed in ancient times, in Stone Age societies, in tribal assemblies, and would also continue to exist once socialism overcame capitalism. We had reached the following conclusion in our debate:

> The generations of Marxists who have lived through the painful experience of fascism and who, on a different scale, have lived through Stalinist degeneration, value the concept of democracy not as something which is in opposition to socialism or communism, but rather as a road towards them *and as a fundamental component of the very same.*

The internal debate had also led us to criticise what was known as the socialist totalitarianism of the Soviet state, not socialist at all. 'Within that State,' we wrote in 1976, 'the Stalinist phenomenon has grown and taken hold, displaying a series of formal characteristics similar to those in fascist dictatorships'. That is to say that our position on democracy was not an opportunistic tactic. It was due to deeply-felt ideological convictions arising from the analysis of an experience we had actually lived through. It led us to confront certain ideas and even so-called principles that the communist movement was deeply attached to, risking a charge of 'heresy'.[17]

Communism in Spain never recovered from the effects of the military veto that reduced its role during the post-electoral phase of the transition and allowed the destructive work of the sectarian groups backed by the leadership of the Soviet Communist Party to flourish, and the so-called Party 'renovators' to grab the limelight.[18] If we had had fifty members of parliament instead of twenty in 1977, these dissident elements would have been re-absorbed. This did not occur and, as a result, the democratic tendencies of the Eurocommunists were defeated and the PCE fell into the hands of people characterised either by their sectarianism or by their ideological and political ambiguity.

On the other hand, Spanish communism underwent an identity crisis following the failure of the Soviet experiment which took the shine off the epoch-making October Revolution. The international communist movement came to an end, with different repercussions depending on the country. In Spain, the PCE has turned the clock back in ideological terms to its sectarian days of isolation[19], prior to the VII Congress of the Communist International and to the Dimitrov-Togliatti unitarian line.[20] Reduced to a small sect, it has opted for camouflaging itself under the mantle of a left-wing coalition – the United Left – but suffers from visible splits due to some remaining factions from the Communist Party.[21] The rest of its component parties lack strength and grass-roots support. Consequently, the sectarian core dominating the remains of the PCE will be the one that determines the course that Izquierda Unida takes.[22]

Is there any future for communism? Firstly, I must explain that when I talk about communism, I do not mean the power system that disintegrated in the Soviet Union, I mean an ideology that does not believe capitalism to be the *non plus ultra* in the evolution of society, but only one stage of a process that is bound to lead to a more egalitarian, democratic society, which we call socialism. In my opinion, this kind of communism does have a great future, whether under that name or any other which is synonymous.

It may be found astonishing that I still express such confidence in the future of the very ideas that are currently contested as never before. It is true to say that neo-liberalism has even made inroads into the Left. For some so-called socialists, being a socialist these days simply means having more social sensitivity, more feelings of solidarity, than the believers in economic liberalism. That is not enough. Being a socialist today as in the past has to mean working towards achieving a society in which the main means of production are commonly owned, or else it means nothing in particular. Whether the strategy employed to achieve this kind of society in the past was the most appropriate and even whether socialism today should be as exclusively and radically class-based as it was in the past, is another matter. In spite of its success, the neo-liberal ideological offensive is running out of steam and has no answer to the major issue of the day, namely structural unemployment. Public opinion has already swung away from pure liberal answers and will one day advocate collective social solutions again.

Notes

1 General Franco continued to refer to the victors and the vanquished in his discourse. In 1958 the National Movement State Party was set up to bring together again under one political roof all those who supported the winning side.
2 Juan Negrín, the Prime Minister, pursued a policy of resistance even after the fall of Catalonia and the collapse in morale on the Republican side, supported by the Communist Party.
3 A Republican colonel, Casado, launched a coup against Negrín's government on 5 March 1939, supported by the PSOE's moderate leader Besteiro and the anarchist CNT, in the hope that by surrendering to Franco better terms could be obtained. Communist troops in Madrid revolted in support of Negrín and were suppressed by Casado, with the loss of about 250 Republican lives. Franco insisted on unconditional surrender, which occurred on 31 March. (Carr, R., *Modern Spain* 1875–1980, Oxford: OUP, 1980, p.152–53.
4 Don Juan, Count of Barcelona, son of the exiled Alfonso XIII and father of Juan Carlos, had liberal leanings.
5 Areilza, the Count of Motrico, a monarchist supporter of Don Juan, became Foreign Minister in the first government of the monarchy (Arias Navarro's last).
6 Carrillo and Suárez held a 'marathon eight-hour meeting' on 27 February 1977 during which in return for legalisation, the former agreed to recognise the monarchy and the monarchist flag (Preston, P., *The triumph of democracy in Spain*, London: Methuen, 1986, p.114).
7 The Constitution stipulates that Spain is a Parliamentary Monarchy and all the King's actions are subject to countersigning (*el refrendo*) by the President of the Congress of Deputies.
8 Founded in September 1976 and led by Manuel Fraga until 1986. 'Refounded' as a mainstream European conservative People's Party (*Partido Popular*) in 1989, led by José María Aznar. In government since 1996.
9 A set of laws which served in lieu of a constitution under the dictatorial regime.
10 As the King's appointee, Suárez had meetings with the opposition before forming the UCD and becoming an elected Prime Minister.

11 The PCE obtained 10 per cent of the vote and 20 out of 350 seats in the lower chamber of deputies in June 1977.

12 The far right newspaper *El Alcázar* noted that 'the consequences would be tragic for Spain. This legalisation has dynamited the 18th of July' and even Fraga's Popular Alliance called the legalisation 'a veritable coup d'état' (Share, D., *The making of Spanish democracy*, New York & London: Praeger, 1986, p.128).

13 A more extensive statement, strongly critical of both Suárez and Gutiérrez Mellado was sent privately to the King (Preston, P., *The triumph of democracy in Spain*, London: Methuen, 1986, p.115).

14 On 14 April the PCE Executive Committee agreed to accept the monarchy and the Spanish flag and on the following day Carrillo confirmed the PCE would accept the rules of parliamentary democracy (Share, *op.cit*, p.129).

15 The electoral system leads to over-representation in parliament of sparsely populated areas, for instance.

16 A debate which led to the notorious expulsion of two leading members who were critical of Carrillo's line, its leading thinker Fernando Claudín and the novelist Jorge Semprún. See Semprún, J., *Autobiografía de Federico Sánchez*, Barcelona: Planeta, 1977.

17 Carrillo published *Eurocomunismo y Estado* in 1977. The Soviets were scandalised and the distance between them grew, acccording to the Mitrokhin Archive (*El País* 26 September 1999, p.24).

18 The author refers to the PCE's internal crisis which began after the 1979 elections and came to a head at the Party's Tenth Congress in 1981. Delegates including Central Committee members, city councillors and public figures criticised Carrillo's leadership style and policies. These 'renovators' gained support from a quarter of the delegates. Afterwards Carrillo pushed through the expulsion of the renovators from the Central Committee, a step which gained national and international notoriety and was followed by a steep decline in the Party's fortunes. See Vega, P. & Erroteta, P., *Los herejes del PCE*, Barcelona: Planeta, 1982; Claudín, F., *Santiago Carrillo*, Barcelona: Planeta, 1983, pp.319–79.

19 He is referring to the Communist International's sectarian 'third period' in which they acted alone, distancing themselves from other parties of the Left. See Sassoon, D., *One Hundred Years of Socialism*, London and New York: I.B.Tauris, p.39.

20 The 1934 decision to encourage Communist parties to form alliances with social-democrats against the fascists. See Hobsbawn, E., *The Age of Extremes: the short twentieth century*, London: Abacus, 1995, p.147–8. Dimitrov was General Secretary of the Communist International and Togliatti the leader of the Italian Communist Party.

21 A reference to the split with Cristina Almeida, a former 'renovator'. She departed in 1998, forming the *Nueva Izquierda* group, allied to the PSOE for the Madrid autonomy elections.

22 Izquierda Unida was led by the communist Julio Anguita from 1989–99 when he was replaced by Francisco Frutos. For the March 2000 elections Frutos made a set of electoral agreements with the PSOE.

Translated by Monica Threlfall.
All footnotes by the editor.

6. The Constitutional Consensus and the Basque Challenge

Gregorio Peces-Barba Martínez

Gregorio Peces-Barba, Doctor of Law, was one of the seven members of the Constitutional Committee of the parliament that drafted the text of the current Spanish Constitution. Born in 1938, he graduated in law from the University of Madrid and in comparative law from Strasbourg. He joined the PSOE in 1972, was Deputy for Valladolid from 1977–86, Parliamentary spokesman for the PSOE and, from 1982–86, President of the Congress of Deputies. He presided over the creation of Carlos III University in Madrid and has been its Rector since 1994. Professor of Philosophy of Law, he is the author of several books on human rights, freedom and power.

When he analysed any legal reality, Jeremy Bentham used to make a distinction between the points of view of the exponent and the critic, separating the internal from the external perspective. Yet whenever I think about the Constitution[1], I am faced with the dilemma of being both an author and a critic, a professor scrutinising a document which is partially his own work. Despite the mild form of schizophrenia this duality induces, I will try to explain what we did and why we did it, and then evaluate the

| CAREFUL! LET'S NOT DROP IT! | LET'S NOT BREAK IT! | IT BELONGS TO ALL OF US! | GOOD WORK, LADS! |

The Constitution is delivered to the President of the Congress by Suárez, González, Carrillo and a reluctant Fraga. By Peridis.

results we achieved. I am reminded of the words with which Jean Jacques Rousseau begins *The Social Contract*:

> If I were asked what entitles me to write about politics, whether I am a prince or a legislator, I would reply neither, and that is precisely why I do write about politics. If I were a prince or a legislator, I would not waste my time saying what has to be done; I would do it or remain silent.[2]

I should also add that when I write about the Constitution, I am putting forward exclusively my own point of view because nowadays I represent only myself as I am no longer a legislator, merely an educator.

I. Drafting the 1978 Constitution

To put the time when the Constitution was drafted into context, it is essential to highlight a series of features that characterised the transition in Spain and the contents of the Constitution itself. The following are worthy of mention:

1. The Constituent Process

The constituent process was possible because of the meeting of minds between public opinion and the democratic opposition on the one hand, and the Monarch and his Prime Minister, Adolfo Suárez, on the other. The disbanding of the *Movimiento* – the state Party – and the official trade unions of the Franco regime, the amnesty, the legalisation of all the political parties and the Law for Political Reform were all indications of that meeting of minds between the winners and losers in our civil war and the younger generation who had not taken part in it. It is worth remembering this because our memories tend to fail us and we sometimes think that the individual and collective freedoms we enjoy have existed since time immemorial.

2. The Inherited Difficulties

Following the elections of 15 June 1977 and the formation of the two parliamentary chambers, the elected Deputies were faced with a constitutional process strewn with difficulties and obstacles, but that also allowed room for hope. The difficulties were inherited from a repressive authoritarian regime which had forbidden the free expression of political pluralism and replaced the complex reality of Spanish society with a construction imposed via a monolithic ideology, although it had already been eroded little by little by the pragmatic developments put into place by technocratic economists working within the regime. Our hope was rooted in the fact that the King and his government, supported by the people, had so far prevented any backlash that could have stopped the elections from taking place. This was, of course, before the failed coup d'état of February 1981.

Furthermore, leaving aside the forty years of dictatorship, from the beginning of the nineteenth century the record of Spanish constitutional history had been bleak. Instability and a lack of constitutional continuity characterised the whole period. Every liberal constitution was replaced by a conservative one, and vice-versa, over and over.

It had proved impossible to maintain any ideological coherence between two consecutive constitutions. The last two, in 1876 and 1931, were the final indication of the lack of communication between the two Spains, and the civil war was the bloody outcome. Even during the Second Republic itself, once the initial euphoria was over, no-one accepted the results of the electoral majorities and launched initiatives such as the October Revolution of 1934, the *Estat Català*[3] and the military uprising of 18 July 1936.

I believe that it is important to point this out since it seems a permanent characteristic of our political behaviour which re-surfaces every once in a while to disrupt our peaceful coexistence. We have displayed an inability to understand what the majority principle means. We manipulate and use it as convenience dictates (and it can be convenient to turn our back on it) without realising that the unilateral breaking of majority agreements, such as a constitutional consensus, can also put the very achievement of its goals at risk. When one of the parties to an agreement, a party important enough to have contributed to a Constitution, severs connections with the nucleus of consensus, out of their own interests and in order to obtain additional advantages that have not been agreed, the others may feel tempted to do the same and, in this way, all progress towards stability and peace is undone.

Spain's history of constitutional instability created an accumulation of pending problems that had never been satisfactorily resolved by any majority, dividing Spanish society and hindering stable coexistence. The question of the form of the State, the regional question, the religious and social questions had set one half of Spain against the other and no satisfactory solutions had ever been found. With its record of liberal revolutions in the nineteenth and twentieth centuries, Spanish history had certainly not managed to become boring, as Montesquieu suggested should be the case for great countries.

3. 'The Message from the Dead'

The 1977 parliament was charged with the historic task of finding a way of overcoming that instability and suggesting appropriate solutions to avoid social and political conflict within a new constitutional framework. In short, we strived to establish some ground rules which would be acceptable to everyone, or at least to the great majority, and which would ensure peace, freedom and democracy and make pluralism and political change possible. It seemed that we all agreed with what President Azaña[4] said in his speech of 18 July 1938 in Barcelona, aimed at future generations, that if Spaniards felt their blood boil once again, they should remember the message from the dead, sent to them from their place of rest in heaven: the eternal verities are peace, compassion and forgiveness.

Fernando de los Ríos[5] had given a similar message on the tragic life of the Spanish polity, advocating harmony and reconciliation, '...See how essential it is that we search the depths of our souls to find the best of our spirit, so that when we turn to Spain, we do not turn to her angry and hateful but, rather, full of love? We must do it to save this land, our begetter, to which I say from the depths of my heart and from this noble and beautiful country: Long live Spain!'[6] It now seems, given later events and the frame of mind we all shared at the time, that the children of both the winners and the losers of our war understood that it was time to overcome hatred and the 'either-friend-or-foe' attitude, which had been instilled in us by Francoist propaganda and by the muzzled institutions that had succumbed to the civil war's evil intent of silencing democratic ideologies and eliminating the people who represented them.

We all realised that it was a special time of generosity, forgiveness and reconciliation. Our common hopes, the joint undertakings of the past, the wish for integration, the ideals of communication and dialogue had to unite us instead of dividing us, overcoming isolationist individualism and real or fictitious mutual grievances. All the exertions of this process, spanning our efforts at integrating Spain while recognising the right to autonomy, our use of the notion of languages as an instrument of communication where there is a common language as well as other voices and a policy of bilingualism[7] – all this could be summed up in the motto of the French philosopher Maritain 'differentiate in order to unite'. In this frame of mind, each parliamentary group, socialists, communists, Catalan nationalists, the new Popular Alliance (AP) and the mixture of old *franquistas*, social-democrats and Christian democrats led by Adolfo Suárez, attempted to achieve a great social pact. Spanish society, equally committed to that long process, followed.

4. Consensus

We were committed to the politics of consensus, to seeking the widest possible agreements from an initial core of UCD and PSOE which was soon extended to include nationalist, communist and later new conservative Deputies. We hammered out a draft of the Constitution with some difficulty and the final text was approved by both Congress and Senate on 31 October 1978, well over a year later.

The parties had four fundamental problems to solve in drafting the Constitution. The first was the religious question, since the dominance of the Catholic church expressed itself in ideological control over the state and the people, leading to the emergence of radical anti-clericalism in reaction to it. The second was the question of peripheral nationalisms. The third related to the form of the state, whether monarchy or republic. Finally, there was the social question, the position of the working class.

Efforts were made to maintain and apply the spirit of frankness and flexibility that had characterised the first part of the transition and had led to the unprecedented historical consensus between opposing political forces. We worked in secret so that the media would have no access to details of the negotiations[8]. Our guiding principle during the bargaining was that there should be no point that was totally unacceptable for any one group. Highly significant mutual concessions were made. The PSOE, for example, gave up their demand with regard to a secular, single school system. This can be clearly seen in Article 27, paragraph 3, which states that, 'The public authorities guarantee the right of parents to have their children receive the religious and moral education corresponding to their own beliefs.'

There were, however, some specific disagreements which almost caused the overall agreement to collapse. Consensus nearly broke down between January and May 1978 after writing the pre-draft because of the question of abortion and the right to life. In part, this was due to the deal between the Deputies, Lavilla of the UCD and Mendizábal of the AP (Popular Alliance), to amend an already negotiated text, preferred by the PSOE and the PCE, which read 'Each *person* has the right to life' (my italics). The Criminal Code states that a newborn baby acquires the rights of a person only twenty-four hours after birth. The manner in which this was drafted would have permitted a subsequent law on abortion. In the end, the UCD decided to amend this piece of text and the PSOE agreed to disagree. Today, Article 15 of the Constitution begins '*Everyone* has the right to life...' (my italics) and anti-abortionists decided to interpret this as if the foetus also had the right to life.[9]

On the other hand, the PSOE had problems in persuading their old militants of the need to recognise the monarchy because of the significance they attached to the republican form of the State and to the resonance of pet phrases such as 'Republic of Workers'. Spanish society should pay tribute to the Crown, the political parties, the unions and, to a lesser extent, the UCD for the efforts they all made in maintaining consensus. The Crown, in particular, accepted the loss of a large part of its status, since it gave up being a *power* of the state to become a mere *organ* of the state.

The roles played by the church, the employers and the military should also be acknowledged since they did not place obstacles in the way of the drafting process. Great value must be placed on the fact that the Constitution eventually stated in Article 16.3 that, 'No religion shall be a state religion' and that the Catholic church, in its relations with the public powers (defined as relations of 'co-operation') would be on an equal footing with the other religions, although the religious beliefs of the Spanish people, most of whom are Catholics, would be taken into account. Those who owned private schools, for example, had to accept that although Article 27 recognised freedom of education, it prohibited the private management of schools and only allowed them ownership, the opposite of what they wanted.

We all had to cut back on our grand programmes and accept wordings that were not totally satisfactory for anyone, yet satisfactory enough for all. Everyone supported the great undertaking apart from insignificant groups on the extreme Left, recalcitrant voices nostalgic for the past on the extreme Right, some sitting 'royal' senators[10] and the Basque Nationalist Party.

5. The Impact of the Basque Problem

The only objective that was not achieved was the support of the Basque nationalists, in spite of the efforts made by everyone which were perhaps disproportionate given that they culminated in the PNV's abstention in the final vote anyway. Article 150, paragraph 2[11] and the First Additional Provision[12] on historic rights were offerings that could not fill their insatiable appetite. Although today they say this is not so, they were never interested in taking part and were satisfied with the tale that Miguel Roca, as the sole representative of the mixed Basque-Catalan parliamentary group, spoke on their behalf. It was better for them to be a sniper on the outside and, while hinting at a compromise which never materialised, to grab as much as possible for their own interests, without any commitment to the common goal. Their strategy was so different from the Catalan nationalists' constructive spirit of collaboration that each side very soon went their own way and Roca gave up trying to represent the Basques.

But the worst difficulties came from outside the parliamentary groups, from the terrorist offensives, particularly on the part of ETA, which punctuated the entire process with horrible, bloody attacks whose effect was solely to provoke a reaction from the military and the security forces. I realised that a firmly established Constitution was going to be very inconvenient for the terrorists, and this intuition has proven to be correct with the passing of time. The Constitution and its values are a reference point for democrats and in times of great tension and difficulty they have drawn the citizens together. On the other hand, if we objectively examine the impact of terrorism and its intellectual, political and electoral supporters, without the passion and prejudice induced by its crimes and useless destruction of lives and families, there can be little doubt that its effectiveness has steadily and visibly diminished.

II. The Functions of a Constitution

Any Constitution should aim at fulfilling three objectives or functions: security, justice and, as a consequence of these, legitimacy.

1. The Function of Security

The function of security, which coincides with what constitutionalists call the 'organic' part, is established by organising the political authorities and institutions, the rules relating to the separation of powers, both functional and territorial, and the different types of regulations, competent bodies and law-making procedures. In this manner, the Constitution restricts power and subjects it to rules and general procedures, known beforehand. It is therefore appropriate to call this the function of security. In this way, Spain is defined as a 'social and democratic State ruled by law', a state organised into 'Autonomous Communities and a parliamentary Monarchy'. In addition, issues such as the financing of the autonomous communities or the electoral system form part of the main constitutional corpus.

There are two important features of Spanish constitutionalism that can be placed in this area, without prejudice to the fact that they could also belong to the function of justice, to which I will refer later. The first is the political form of the State and the other is what was formerly called the regional question. In both cases, the constitutional answers are prudent and pacificatory – the result of the grand general agreement called the consensus.

a) The definition of the State as a parliamentary monarchy was the result of an agreement in which the parties on the Left gave up their republican position to support the monarchy as a body symbolising the unity and permanence of the State, in return for the Crown relinquishing its privileges and representing neither executive, nor legislative, nor judicial power; that is, losing its real *potestas* (power) in order to gain *auctoritas* (authority). The Left sacrificed what until then had been part of their intellectual or moral heritage, and the King relinquished his position as a state power. It took some effort for republican ideals to be shelved, particularly for those people who had lived through the failed Second Republic and had been persecuted for that noble cause. They sacrificed ideals and hopes as well as due reparations. The King sacrificed his status with laudable lucidity, because he could only have kept it through force. Everyone was generous, setting aside grievances or choosing to give up certain powers in return for creating a new form of the State, which was to have legitimacy both in its inception, its formulations and its practice.

With the passing of time, the King has effectively consolidated his legitimacy by properly carrying out his functions and duties. In the early days his legitimacy was much more rational than historical, that is to say, it derived from the new Constitution not from monarchical tradition. But it was considerably strengthened by virtue of being put to the test, both on occasions such as the night of 23 February 1981, and in the King's day to day behaviour, where he carried out his constitutional duties without overstepping them. It is interesting to note the impact of this type of monarchy (which enjoys no privileges or prerogatives) on a parliamentary system and on the representation of sovereignty (which resides exclusively with parliament), in contrast to the difficulties experienced with shared sovereignty in republics, where the Head of State and the parliament are both elected by universal suffrage, as in Portugal or France. Such a comparison increases the worth of our configuration of the Crown, since it reverses the relationship that existed in the nineteenth century when monarchies shared privileges with parliament. Shared privileges between the Head of State and the parliament in republics creates tensions because responsibilities are split and a struggle for power ensues. Placing the representation of sovereignty exclusively in the hands of Parliament avoids these conflicts, which particularly arise in republics when the two positions in which sovereignty resides can be held by leaders who belong to opposing ideologies.

b) With regard to the State of Autonomous Communities, the Constitution clearly delimits the relevant areas for establishing such Communities – contrary to many ill-founded opinions – although it does leave the way open for further political decisions to be made in subordinate hierarchical fields, regarding for instance the actual Statutes of Autonomy[13] and other highest order organic laws. The relevant points in the constitutional consensus on this matter, in the social pact which is at the heart of our coexistence, are the following:

i) Exclusive nationalism is rejected, whether it be Spanish nationalism that denies the existence of cultural nations within the boundaries of Spain such as Catalonia, the Basque Country or Galicia, or peripheral nationalism that denies the existence of the Spanish nation and the possible inclusion of their own community within it, on the basis of their claim to 'difference'.

ii) From this perspective, the defence of Spain as a nation is compatible with the acknowledgement of nationalities and cultural regions within its borders, and their distinctive identities. In the eyes of the Constitution, therefore, Spain is a nation comprising nationalities and regions although the only sovereign nation is the Spanish nation. We carefully considered the wording of the Constitution on this matter. It was thus perfectly clear that national sovereignty resided with the Spanish as a people and that the powers of the State originated exclusively from them as a collective (as stated in Article 1.2). Similarly, the format used by Article 3 regarding languages was based on the same philosophy. Article 3 states that Castilian is the 'official Spanish language of the State' and that 'the other Spanish languages' are 'also official within the respective Autonomous Communities in accordance with their Statutes'. This was a way of including linguistic pluralism without creating non-existent 'facts'; of regulating pluralism there where it did exist by making bilingualism a rule and a principle for its official institutions. The problem of language is not a fundamental point but rather an institutional principle or guarantee to protect bilingualism. The subjective right to use a language of one's choice arises only as a result of that principle, together with the obligation that everyone has to know Castilian (as stated in Article 3.1).

The only 'distinctive features' of territories within the state of Spain (or 'differential facts' – *hechos diferenciales* as the nationalists call them) which are recognised in the framework of the Constitution refer to language, culture and regional laws and have no constitutional significance beyond this. This means that they do not justify any kind of original sovereignty of the territories where they exist, nor can they be used to gain qualitative differences with regard to the other Autonomies. Murcia, Castilla-León or Madrid do not have a linguistic identity distinct from the common language of all Spaniards, but this cannot mean that they are put at a disadvantage in any way, such as regards the recognition of their institutions. Having their own language does not grant Catalonia, Galicia or the Basque Country any different status with respect to their powers, other than in the linguistic field itself, which now enjoys a constitutional protection which it previously lacked. Nor can this difference be alleged to claim different and wider-ranging powers in the areas of health, the media or social security.

iii) The State of Autonomous Communities is functionally (in practice) a federal state and it is therefore nonsense to argue that Spain should now become a federal state. As far as it is possible, it already is; it cannot become so by constructing a notion of original sovereignty in some Autonomous Communities, because the Constitution cannot amend reality retroactively, it can only try to improve it for the future.

2. The Justice Function

The Constitution in its justice function, which coincides with what constitutionalists call the 'dogmatic' part, formally sets out the broad outlines of a codified public ethics, in the form of higher values, principles and rights. This material content, together with the formal content described under its security function, provides a framework for legislative and executive law-making which is of a lower order than the Constitution itself. The fact that higher values are formulated in the Constitution as a public ethics creates a relationship between policy-making and the judiciary. The allocation of the principles relating to execution, law-making and interpretation to separate bodies (the division of powers) contributes to the smooth operation of the constitutional order and to the application of the law. Finally, the system of fundamental citizenship rights (Title I) and the specific guarantees given to citizens[14], in particular the right to appeal for their enforcement, means that aspects of public morality are formulated as individual rights that are readily accessible and actionable by individuals. It is also clear that this broad framework of a codified public ethics enables them to be guaranteed via the Constitutional Tribunal.[15]

Let us now look at how a consensus was reached on the two other areas which have been fraught with conflicts throughout Spain's history and remain largely unresolved. They can be located more or less within the Constitution's function of justice: the religious question and the social question.

2.1. The Religious Question

Throughout its modern history, fierce religious intransigeance closed Spain off from any dissident faith and led to the persecution of non-Catholic believers and the entrenchment of a state religion for long periods, which generated deep-seated anti-clerical feelings in reaction. This antagonism was one of the major underlying causes of the civil war, which the church declared to be a Christian crusade but during which many priests and members of religious orders were murdered, particularly in the republican zone. To put an end to such emnity, the new Constitution organised the church-state relationship from a new perspective, giving special consideration to the legacy of the war.

The broad outlines of the constitutional settlement therefore include the following:

i) The principle of a secular State, where no religion can be a state religion.
ii) Ideological and religious freedom together with freedom of worship as fundamental rights.
iii) The privacy of a person's beliefs in order to guarantee freedom of thought. No-one is obliged to declare their beliefs.
iv) Co-operation of the State with the Catholic church and other religions within the bounds of a secular State. This means that such co-operation cannot be used to covertly re-establish a State religion.

It is important to note that other areas, for instance the specific relations of the State with the Catholic church, are dealt with in the Concordats between the Kingdom of Spain and the Holy See, which were drawn up before the Constitution was written. In contrast, all the current agreements with other churches and religions were made after the Constitution. It is worth noting that in recent years the church has launched an offensive to recover lost ground in the fields of religious education, the universities and society in general.

2.2. The Social Question

The 1978 Constitution adopts a very clear position with regard to the social question by defining the State as a social and democratic State ruled by law. The following provisions can be highlighted:

i)   The recognition of the prominent roles played by the workers' trade unions and the employers' associations (Article 7).

ii)   The recognition of the right to belong to a trade union and the right to strike (Article 28).

iii) The dignity of the individual is, amongst other factors, the basis for social peace (Article 10.1).

iv)   The recognition of the right to education, which shall be obligatory and free (Articles 4 and 27.1).

v)   The duty of the authorities to promote the necessary conditions and to remove any obstacles to ensure that freedom and equality are real and effective (Article 9.2).

vi)   The duty of all to contribute to sustain public spending, according to their means, through the tax system (Article 31.1).

vii) The right to private property has a social function and can be subordinated to the public interest (Articles 33 and 128).

viii) The right of labour to collective bargaining and the binding force of collective agreements (Article 37).

ix)   The authorities shall provide social protection for the family and children (Article 39).

x)   The authorities shall maintain a public system of social security for all citizens (Article 41).

xi)   The protection of health is recognised as a right (Article 43).

xii) The authorities shall carry out rehabilitation and integration policies for the disabled (Article 49).

xiii) The authorities shall guarantee adequate pensions to the elderly (Article 50).

xiv) The country's entire wealth is subordinate to the general interest (Article 128).

All these points lead us to conclude that the Spanish Constitution approaches these questions with the goal of seeking a basic social homogeneity. Hermann Heller called this a 'social state'[16] and Fernando de los Ríos, in his book *The humanist meaning of socialism*, called it 'social constitutionalism'[17]. These constitutional provisions are doubtless a firm brake on ultra-liberal and economics-driven ideologies as well as on the philosophy of the minimal State which have in recent times become a fundamentalist credo, like so many others at different points in history.

3. The Legitimacy Function

The function of legitimacy arises as a consequence of the security and justice functions. The Constitution must answer two key questions: 'Who is in control?' and 'How are orders to be given?', identifying the institutions, the powers and the laws emanating from them. Through the justice function the constitution-makers replied to the question 'What are we ordered to do?' by expressing the higher values, principles and rights which allow the political and legal morality of the Spanish system to be identified. The legitimacy function in the Constitution takes these answers into account and also provides the answer to two further questions: 'Why are the orders given?' and 'Why does one obey?' that is, it accounts for the elements in the Constitution which allow one to make judgements about the origin of power, about its exercise, and about the sources of the body of laws and their interpretation and application. In effect, the great constitutional consensus underlying the text of 1978, the regular call to elections and political action, the widespread exercise of rights and freedoms and the daily flow of legal appeals made by individuals claiming their constitutional rights are all a clear sign that citizens and the general public value the system positively and believe it to be legitimate.

Aside from that, there is a political force that is radically opposed to our constitutional model and expresses itself through the terrorist violence of ETA. The potent outcry on the part of the vast majority of our citizens against its crimes not only signifies a rejection of this irrational and brutal manner of dealing with political problems, but also, paradoxically, signifies the Constitution's legitimacy. For what impels citizens to unite in massive demonstrations is, at root, an outpouring of constitutional values. It is very significant that any calls made to bring back capital punishment on these occasions have been roundly rejected by the majority of people. Not even their anger and other similar feelings can make the public change its opinion over capital punishment, abolished by the Constitution (Article 15).

III. The Constitution in its Third Decade

If we look back over the two decades that the Constitution has been in force, some strengths and some weaknesses become apparent, although, on balance, it is a good law. It is generally effective and widely accepted. It is even used by those who did not accept it at the time: Herri Batasuna has recourse to it for its own defence, which is significant. Fundamental rights are protected in Spain; the armed forces have been brought under the control of civilian power and the courts now act independently.[18] Secularism has developed and permeated society in general, making Spain a secular country. Stable majorities for government are formed through the electoral system and collaboration in Parliament, and governments are durable. The 'State of Autonomous Communities' has developed at a reasonable pace, although there are some latent risks in this connection which will be examined below.

In my view, difficulties continue to exist in two of the key areas examined above: the religious question and the regional question.

1. The Resurgence of Clericalism

Firstly, there has been a return to what could be called 'clericalism', on the back of some doctrinal statements made by the Catholic church such as the 1990 bishops' document (*The truth will make us free*). It reflected John Paul II's idea of bringing the church and society more into line with one another, as if both were governed by a natural order equivalent to an absolute truth that must take precedence over political majorities, merely because these are transient. Under this doctrinal influence, some Catholic authorities believe, for example, that parliament cannot legislate on abortion. Another illustration of such clericalism is the bishops' plans to create new church-controlled universities in Avila and Cartagena – perhaps in response to the boom in state universities and the problems suffered by the private ones. The Council of State[19], however, has refused to approve them. A clerical influence on the government of the Partido Popular can also be detected.

2. The Basque Enigma

At the turn of the millennium the Spanish polity is still faced with a number of political dilemmas that the Basque nationalist democrats have not helped to resolve. In particular, the 1998 document presented by José María Ardanza when he was *Lehendakari* (leader of the Basque Country) went no way towards enlightening us. Instead, he created new doubts as to the programmatic horizon on which democratic nationalists base themselves.[20] Do they understand self-determination to be an exclusive decision to be taken by Basque citizens, ignoring the ground rules established in the Constitution? Is it a new twist on the pact that Basque towns had with the Crown in the old days? Is it independence? In any case, the vagueness and ambiguity of these goals makes any solution enormously difficult. Basque citizens have a very broad-ranging Autonomy Statute and a level of self-government not enjoyed by any other European region. It is therefore not at all clear what can be offered to those responsible for the violence in return for them to stop killing. Any concession to their demands would mean accepting that their murders, kidnappings and extortion had bent the will of the majority to theirs.

Is there any similarity between the aims of the separatists and those of the Basque nationalist democrats? It is surprising that a party with an undoubted record of resistance to dictatorship, such as the PNV, should accept that its long-term strategy should be pursued in a context where only violence would bring concessions. When all is said and done, making headway in this manner, before the terrorists give up their weapons, means exempting them from their crimes, something that no civilised society can reasonably accept because if violence achieves results then anyone could be tempted to use it for their own ends.

Still, nationalist parties have only a slim majority in the Basque Country and they have repeatedly stated that they do not accept the Spanish nation and do not feel themselves to be Spaniards.[21] The Constitution protects their freedom because one cannot put up border controls for beliefs, nor police ideas, so they have the right to hold such views. They should use their freedom to convince the majority, under the same ground rules as everyone else. Instead, they repeatedly give in to the temptation of holding talks with the men of violence, thereby obtaining advantages for their own brand of nationalism, in exchange for peace and an end to the violence. This is not political fair play.

The Basque democratic nationalists should come to a decision. It is becoming unsustainable for them to defend democratic values (which they have always supported) while maintaining contact with Herri Batasuna[22], because they deploy the politics of hate and promote narrow friend-or-foe polarisation – the very antithesis of democratic values. Furthermore, it is ever harder to grasp why the PNV places greater importance on rejecting the Spanish Constitution than on rejecting violence and death, and why the nationalist identity that unites them to Herri Batasuna should take priority over the defence of freedom and democracy that separates them.

3. The Law on Language Policy

Once a stable and reliable party to the consensus, the Catalan nationalists have set alarm bells ringing with their 'normalisation' of the Catalan language[23], the result of a certain obsession attributed particularly to President Pujol himself. For it raises issues of constitutional loyalty. Their general aim is correct and can be shared, given that the Catalan language was first persecuted and then ignored during the Franco years. But they display a barely restrained tendency to impose rather unreasonable demands on, and even to break with, the constitutional consensus on bilingualism. An example of this can be found in Law 1/98 of 7 January on language policy. For the first time a law has created real tension in an open and tolerant society such as Catalonia. It signifies a shift in the nationalists' understanding of languages, for it grants excessive and unconstitutional prominence to the notion of an 'own' language, which is used to argue that Catalan should be the only language of all institutions. It definitively buries the constitutional provision that Catalan and Castillian shall be co-official in Catalonia.

4. The Great Value of the Original Consensus

These matters make us reflect on the meaning of that great social pact known as the consensus. The key to finding the answers lies in understanding the profound value of that consensus. Consensus means much more than a simple exchange of mutual interests, in an unstable equilibrium, or a kind of haggling that can be shifted *à la carte* to cover whichever interests come to the fore with the passing of time. Consensus is much more than an agreement for a fixed period. Above all there can be no unilateral exit for one of the parties to the original consensus, for any political 'departure' cannot but have consequences for the others. When the Catholic church or other participants in the consensus, be they nationalists or the United Left front, raise new issues that were not considered twenty years ago in the Constitution, they cannot expect that this will not create uneasiness or be disagreed with. Nor, of course, can they take any such responses to be a snub to their position.

Nor can the constitutional consensus be at the mercy of short-lived majorities reflecting the changing whims of the public, in the same way as consumer tastes change, one day being enthused by a product and the next, dropping it. In this way, the abolition of capital punishment cannot depend on whether there are many terrorist attacks or few, nor on any unfortunate court judgement which most people happen to disapprove of. Equally, the consensus cannot be re-interpreted to fit a particular party's immediate need for parliamentary support, to fit the results of a survey of public opinion, or the interest of a certain pressure group aligned to a particular party in power. For all these reasons, a change in the way in which the Autonomous Communities are financed cannot derive from a simple agreement between the government of the day and its political allies if all the parties to the consensus do not agree, because this is a matter affecting all the constitutional parties. Finally, people who have shown disdain for the values protected in the consensus or who hold opinions that openly contradict it, cannot occupy prominent public positions, whether military posts, Attorney-General or Governor of the Bank of Spain, or be appointed to them.

On the contrary, our profound respect for the constitutional consensus should derive equally from the historic problems it has surmounted and from an awareness that it is required, unavoidably, to ensure peaceful co-existence. Past events should not be forgotten, which is why irresponsible attempts unilaterally to amend the Constitution, in the belief that no ill effects will result, cannot be countenanced. The nationalists should abandon resorting to the fictitious grievances and unwaivable claims that they place on the table one after the other. And the Catholic church should desist from trying to recover spheres of influence that are incompatible with the secular nature of the State, and from invoking 'holy', unquestionable truths to counter the majority principle and other rules of the democratic system. Such unreasonable behaviour is not only undesirable because it rekindles its own dormant opponents who then rise up, inflamed, in the shape of an exclusivist Spanish nationalism or a similarly unjustified anti-clericalism. It is also undesirable because such behaviour disregards the very diagnosis of Spain's historic evils which the constitutional consensus judiciously aimed to eliminate.

The consensus that brought our constitutional process to a successful conclusion did not mean that any comprehensive philosophy had triumphed, nor that any particular idea of the common good had gained the upper hand. Rather, it involved a compact between a plurality of ideas that were compatible with the rules of the game outlined in the Constitution. At that time, a legitimate majority accepted its political and legal values, its position on public ethics, on how the state should be organised and how powers should be distributed between public bodies and institutions. These were believed to be reasonable and provided a minimum basis for agreement in a pluralist society. All parties to the consensus publicly acknowledged at that time that the constitutional rules were able to protect individual rights as well as the claims to distinct identities, particularly those made with respect to the use of the other languages of Spain, besides providing the greatest security, freedom, equality and cooperation possible for everyone, while respecting the rights of others. As an official declaration, supported by an overwhelming parliamentary and public majority, the Constitution implies a moral and political commitment which no participant can wriggle out of without facing doubts about their trustworthiness and incurring consequences for political stability.

All the parties to that social and political contract owe fidelity to its rules as it constitutes a pact for co-existence which harmonises different and sometimes opposing interests so as to encourage them to avoid engaging in mutual destruction. The rules were not imposed on us – we voluntarily accepted them and the limitations they placed on each party's long-term programmes. These restrictions were freely taken on as an expression of the desire to live together along non-authoritarian principles. Those who were party to it must refrain from seeking to achieve their long-term aims if these are not compatible with the commitments agreed to in the consensus. Only by maintaining the basic agreement that the Constitution represents can ensure that the values and interests that made us all accept it at the time continue to be safeguarded in a lasting and stable fashion.

5. *Amending the Text of the Constitution*

All this is not to say that the actual text of the Constitution cannot be amended but that any amendment must be made with the agreement of all and out of the conviction that it is advantageous for everyone and that it maintains the original political equilibrium. On no account can terrorist violence be the catalyst for constitutional reform, for there is no logical or moral link between the two. It would anyway be a concession to the worst kind of utilitarianism that even Jeremy Bentham[24] would never have defended. Any reform must be undertaken for justified and rational reasons, rather than be inspired by fear or even the desire to put an end to fear, however worthy this may be. Reform must emerge from dialogue, which is incompatible with a climate of violence that disrupts the exchange of views necessary to freely reach a conclusion. The Spanish people deserve a solid rational basis for any alteration to the Constitutional consensus. Therefore it should take place under the same procedural conditions as the original one, since these allowed the aim of peace and reconciliation to be entertained. Any additional text can only be produced through the 'public use of reason' as Habermas says.[25] In conclusion, I declare that the constitutional consensus is a pact which, as it stands, can reasonably expect endorsement by free and equal citizens, both on account of the historic moment in which it was written, and of the principles for co-existence which it contains.

Notes

1   Peces-Barba, Gregorio, *La Constitución española de 1978: un estudio de derecho y política*, (with Prieto Sanchís, L.). Valencia: Fernando Torres, 1981; and *La elaboración de la Constitución de 1978*, Madrid: Centro de Estudios Constitucionales, 1988.

2   Rousseau, Jean Jacques, *The Social Contract*, first published 1762. Translated from the original French reprinted in Rousseau, Du contrat social, Paris: Flammarion, 1966 – Ed.

3   Estat Catalá was a Catalan nationalist party, the hard-line separatist wing of the Esquerra Republicana de Catalunya in the 1930s. Its leader, Josep Dencàs took the group in a fascist direction and pushed for a separatist rebellion in October 1934. See Preston, Paul, *La destrucción de la democracia en España*, Madrid: Ediciones Turner, 1978 – Ed.

4   Manuel Azaña (1880–1940), the 'father' of the Second Republic, was head of government from 1931–3 and head of the winning Popular Front coalition of 1936. After three months as Prime Minister he became President of the Republic in May 1936 and remained in Spain during the civil war until February 1939 when he went into exile in France – Ed.

5   A leader of the PSOE, minister in the Republican government of 1931–3, academic and socialist thinker – Ed.

6   See his lecture 'Sentido y significación de España' given in Mexico at the Círculo Pablo Iglesias on 17 January 1945, in de los Ríos, Fernando, *Escritos sobre democracia y socialismo*, ed. by Zapatero, Virgilio, Madrid: Taurus, 1975. Also in Volume V, p.342 of his *Obras Completas*, ed. by Rodríguez de Lecea, Teresa, Antropos, Fundación Caja Madrid, 1997.

7   See the excellent book by López García, Angel, *El rumor de los desarraigados: Conflicto de lenguas en la península ibérica*, Barcelona: Anagrama, 2nd ed., 1991.

8   Though, perhaps inevitably, a draft of the text was leaked to a magazine – Ed.

9   AP later appealed the 1983 abortion law before the Constitutional Tribunal on these grounds – Ed.

10 The 1977 parliament still had 41 senators appointed by King Juan Carlos – Ed.

11 Article 150:2 states that the state may transfer or delegate powers to the Autonomous Communities and that a subsequent law would provide the corresponding financial resources as well as establish the forms of control reserved for the State – Ed.

12 Stipulates that the Constitution will protect and respect the historic rights of the old 'self-governing' territories – those which had previously been granted their own laws – Ed.

13 The Statute of an Autonomous Community is its constitution – Ed.

14 The first part (Title I) of the Constitution sets out the fundamental rights and duties of citizens in Articles 1–52. Articles 53–54 refer to the guarantees given by public powers that these will be effectively actionable in law, i.e. binding. To ensure this, citizens have the right of appeal to the Constitutional Tribunal and the Defender of the People (Ombudsman) – Ed.

15 The Constitutional Tribunal's main function is to pass judgement on whether a new law is in keeping with the Constitution or violates it – Ed.

16 Heller, Hermann, *Teoría del Estado*, Mexico: Fondo do Cultura Económica, 1942, ninth printing, 1984; and *Escritos Políticos*, Madrid: Alianza, 1985.

17 de los Ríos, Fernando, *El sentido humanista del socialismo*, Madrid: Morata, 1926; new edition edited by Díaz, Elías, Madrid: Castalia, 1976.

18 Although the independence of the judiciary continues to be one of the most contested issues of Spanish democracy.

19 The Council of State, the highest advisory body with constitutional status, advises the government and autonomous communities on a wide range of administrative and legal matters in order to pre-empt litigation at a later stage (Newton, M, *The institutions of modern Spain: a political and economic guide*, Revised edition 1997: p87) – Ed.

21 The Ardanza Plan envisaged a dialogue between Basque paties which would include Herri Batasuna once ETA declared an indefinite ceasefire. But by the end of 1998, the PNV had signed up to the Declaration of Lizarra promoted by Herri Batasuna which asserted the Basque right to self-determination. See Gillespie, Richard, 'Peace moves in the Basque Country', *Journal of Southern Europe and the Balkans*, Vol.1 (2), November 1999 – Ed.

21 See for instance, Javier Arzalluz's interview in *El País*, 17 May 1998 – Ed.

22 Herri Batasuna, now presenting itself to election as Euskal Herria, is the party which defends ETA's line – Ed.

23 'Normalisation' (from 'norm', not 'normal') refers to the title of the law passed by the Catalan parliament, making it 'the norm' to use Catalan, as opposed to merely being 'co-official' with Castilian – Ed.

24 Jeremy Bentham (1748–1832) British philosopher and economist, exponent of the utilitarian school of thought.

25 This was the original title of Habermas's *Politischer Liberalismus*, Frankfurt am Main: Suhrkamp, 1996.

Translation by Kathryn Phillips-Miles and Monica Threlfall

7. To Reform or not to Reform the Constitution? A Catalan view*

Miquel Roca Junyent

Miguel Roca was one of the seven members of the Spanish parliament's constitutional committee which drafted the current Spanish Constitution. Born in 1940 in France, the son of Republican exiles, he graduated in law from the University of Barcelona in 1961 and became active in anti-Francoist politics. A leader of the revival of political nationalism in Catalonia, he came to prominence on addressing the crowds openly celebrating Catalonia's national day (Diada) in 1976, the first time since the civil war. A Deputy in Congress for the Catalan Convergence and Union Party (1977–85), for he was one of the authors of Catalonia's own Statute of Autonomy. In the mid-eighties he headed an initiative to unite political centrists with moderate nationalists across Spain. Currently practising and teaching law, he presides the Social Council of the Polytechnic University of Catalonia.

A new topic of public debate has been launched in Spain: constitutional reform. The arguments have become quite radical in the heat of controversy and some people present the 1978 Constitution as outdated, the product of a time in history no longer viewed positively. These critics see the transition as being fraught with mistakes, oversights and failures of nerve. For them, the Constitution is simply the outcome of questionable behaviour, which has served neither to solve nor to contain Spain's real problems.

It should come as no surprise then that, ever since these thoughts began to be voiced, aided and abetted by the twentieth anniversary of the 1978 Constitution, I should wish to reiterate my defence of a text that has provided the background to the longest period of democratic normality in the history of Spain. It is a straightforward and unrestrained defence. I believe that in 1978 we defined, between all of us, a good regulatory framework for co-existence in freedom, and I believe that this framework is still valid, not just because it has a meaning in law, but mainly because it has become firmly rooted in the collective consciousness of the vast majority of citizens who identify with what the Constitution has represented until now and still represents: a guarantee for the future.

* A Spanish version of this article was published in *Veinte años después: la Constitución cara al siglo XXI*, Madrid: Taurus.

Such a defence does not prevent me from admitting that there are some sections of our Constitution that could be improved, some that could be omitted and others that could be added. A constitution, however, is far more than just a series of articles strung together; taken as a whole it reflects a spirit, a collective will. Some astute constitutional lawyers and commentators may criticise the draftsmanship and complain about oversights, gaps, contradictions, ambiguities and vagueness, but that is not an obstacle to now giving a highly positive assessment to a document that has presided over more than twenty *exceptional* years of political co-existence, with no dictatorships, military uprisings, states of emergency or suspensions of freedoms.

The possibility of revising it one day should not be denied, but rather demystified. It should not be viewed as traumatic since the Constitution itself makes provision for it. But saying that revision is not tantamount to breaking a sacrament is not the same as saying that it is advisable. To be perfectly frank, I strongly believe that now is not the time to embark upon a process of constitutional reform. I believe in the currency and validity of the model defined in 1978 and also that, with sufficient political will, new possibilities can be found in the text in order to solve some of the problems that its critics are pointing to. When I state that *there is no urgent reason* to undertake constitutional reform at the moment, I am referring to substantial amendments that go beyond specific small revisions.

Indeed, by making use of the same consensus that presided over the drafting of the Constitution, amendments could be made relating to matters such as the Senate which, as is generally agreed, has proved rather ineffective as a chamber representing the regions of Spain.[1]

Having set out my initial approach, the article will proceed as follows. Firstly, I will argue for the continued relevance of the values that made it possible to draft the Constitution. Secondly, I will examine the problems that are currently being attributed to the nature of the Constitution's development, particularly regarding the Autonomous Communities. Finally, I will conclude by considering the factors that should complete and complement the framework of the 1978 Constitution in the light of a political situation emerging over twenty years later.

I. Drafting the Constitution

The Constitution was not the result of an academic or theoretical endeavour. We, the participants, were not a group of professors cloistered in some seminary, appointed to draft a Constitution independently of what was demanded by the social and political realities of the time. On the contrary, all our work on the Constitution solemnly expressed the values that the democratic transition brought to the fore and wished to enshrine. The 1978 Constitution *could not have been any different* from what it was. Perhaps some details could have been drafted a shade differently but, as a whole, the Constitution reflected the will of the great majority of the people.

The overlap between constitution-drafting and the transition process provided the text with one of its essential features: it is the result of *consensus*. Yet according to some, this seems to be one of its weak points. They now claim that consensus weakened the coherence of its provisions and that an excessive desire for consensus resulted in ambiguity. Again, it should come as no surprise that I still defend the premise that the desire for consensus was the winning card of the transition and the best foundation for any process of regime change.

On the one hand, consensus was the alternative to a 'take it or leave it' approach. No-one wanted a Constitution that a majority forced on a minority. Rather, everyone was to feel comfortable within a framework for relationships that was being defined. Consensus meant breaking with the tradition of intolerance, intransigence and fratricidal confrontation that had characterised both recent and contemporary Spanish history. Consensus meant opting for agreement and dialogue; it meant putting all one's eggs into the basket of co-existence in freedom, and putting up with the sometimes difficult duty to respect one's adversaries instead of savouring the bitter taste of despising them.

On the other hand, consensus obliged us to transact bargains. The recurrent 'all or nothing' postures of the past had to be buried and a new value was placed on the meeting points around which a shared vision could be established between opposing positions, on the basis of reciprocal concessions. It was not just a question of making democratic pluralism possible, but also a question of giving preference to pact and agreement. It was not enough to recognise diversity – there was a desire to move forward together onto common ground.

And all this was achieved. Democracy was consolidated in Spain in spite of the bad omens. Despite those who forecast that Spain would be unable to recognise her own pluralism, progress was made towards the present State of Autonomous Communities – the most radical process of decentralisation of political power witnessed in post-war Europe – which reversed more than two hundred and fifty years of homogenising and de-personalising centralism. Spain is enjoying the longest period of democratic stability in her history.

The results are so obvious that we do not need to be reminded of them. Only deliberately perverse or ignorant observers would dispute the statement that the 1978 Constitution laid the foundations for a democratic and strongly decentralised state. Moreover, the whole process in many cases exceeded the expectations of those who were most deeply involved in the constituent process, as for some, the coup d'état on 23 February 1981 was much more in line with what they had expected than the failure of the coup itself and the democratic consolidation which followed it.

II. Twenty Years On

By 1998, however, consensus was no longer in fashion. Some believe that it was useful for a specific period in our history, but that once democracy was established, the game of majorities and minorities[2] should have replaced the requirement of consensus. Obviously there is some truth in this, but it is also true – at least for me – that other powerful reasons could be used to defend the need to resort to consensus once again as the main, though not exclusive, cornerstone of the rules of our democratic co-existence.

Firstly, let us recognise that a Constitution born out of consensus politics is less resistant after the practice is abandoned. Our Constitution was not only created out of a consensus but also aimed to further it. We did not come up with a stop-gap answer to a passing situation, we envisaged a new way of understanding democracy in Spain.

We did not want democracy to be simply majority government won through democratic and free elections, we wanted a type of power that would display due respect for the minority, never forgetting for a moment the values of pluralism and freedom. We desire democracy in order to enjoy it together for the greatest possible length of time. Consensus offered the best guarantee of democratic sustainability.

As a result, our Constitution seems to co-exist uneasily with periods of radicalisation and tension. Its institutions do not prosper under excessive confrontation. It was deliberately designed as a kind of constitution-with-conditions that not only defined the rules of the game but also imposed a style which, if it is not followed, makes it difficult to operate the system itself.

Was this a whim on the part of the drafting committee? Clearly not. The members were aware that the challenge facing Spain was not only to win freedom but mainly to live in freedom. Consensus was required as something that should always pervade important decisions in order to leave behind our past tradition of frustrated hopes. Even now, we all know that a couple of decades is too short a time for us to be able to say the battle is over. From an institutional perspective democracy is now consolidated, but more time is needed for democratic values to become deeply entrenched in our customs in such a way as to allow us to experience them as part of our identity, as simply the way we are.

Secondly, consensus can be defended as the means for future progress in Spain. Contemporary society is built on the basis of identity within diversity and multiculturalism. It is the kind of society that perceives fundamentalism as a simplistic outlook, backward-looking and leading to poverty. The Western world is learning that progress cannot be made through intransigence or 'take it or leave it' attitudes, as if everything were black and white. Progress shows up in muted colours, in integrating syntheses, in compromises and compacts. Little by little, everyone around us is learning that the truth is multi-faceted, that there are different ways of seeing it and that there may be positive elements in all these different ways of being which are well worth taking account of. Spanish society made this discovery still rather recently.

The great democracies can boast of wide arenas of political action which enjoy a general acceptance by most political and social forces. For them it is never a question of changing everything, but only of modifying some detail where a disagreement does not affect the general interest. The general interest should be a value taken on board whenever possible by a wide majority, surpassing the strictly party-political. For being able to claim an extensive area of consonance over fundamental issues does not make political debate any less interesting, it simply forces politicians to discover new ambitions, to propose new targets and generate fresh hopes for such a vastly more complex society.

I believe therefore that a basic consensus about how to live in a democracy, and over the values which are accorded total respect, empowers society and the political system. To my understanding, this was the purpose with which the designers wished to endow the 1978 Constitution: to make the consensus that engendered it last for as long as it remained in force and even preside over any reform or amendment. So it comes as no surprise that the debate on amending the Constitution has appeared whenever the political consensus has deteriorated. As soon as it is rebuilt, talk of constitutional reform feels less compelling.

The Constitution's Limitations

It the light of the above points, let us discuss the limitations currently attributed to the text of the Constitution. In the main, the debate has polarised around the evolution of Spain's quasi-federal State of Autonomous Communities. Some argue that it was a mistake to construct it, being both unnecessary and dangerous. They see progress on autonomy as a clear threat to the unity of the nation. Others view it as a structure that does not solve the age-old dilemma of how to make Spain function as a pluri-national entity. Altogether there is a wide range of views criticising the practical consequences of the constitutional provisions regarding the Autonomous Communities – too often without offering good reasons.

In recent times events such as ETA's truce have increased the controversy.[3] Wide-ranging and contradictory theories can be read and heard on proposed constitutional reforms that serve either to satisfy or to oppose nationalist claims. I do not intend to become involved in this controversy, but the following points may help to define its parameters. For a start, there are four statements that no-one should dispute:

1. Spain today enjoys a significant decentralisation of political power, which has nothing to envy the federal system of, say, Germany, in general terms.
2. The Autonomous Communities enjoy a significant level of powers which in the case of Catalonia represent its highest level of self-government experienced since 1714. The Basque Country enjoys a level of self-government not seen in any German *land*.
3. No other European or Western country has gone through such a rapid and peaceful process of decentralising political power.
4. The structure of the Autonomous Communities has raised far fewer operational problems than expected, especially considering that the state into which it was introduced was highly centralised yet has been partially dismembered, not after any revolution, but following a succession of implants of the new autonomous structures, yet without the complete disappearance of some very typical features of the centralist state.

All this means that we can be very pleased with the way the Constitution has developed with regard to regional autonomy. However, such satisfaction should be compatible with the will to proceed further.

Reforming the Constitution?

Some Autonomous Communities, particularly Catalonia and the Basque Country, accept that they enjoy a high level of self-government while still evidencing their wish to achieve an even higher level. The question is whether their wishes can be fulfilled within the current framework of the Constitution. Some politicians base their demands for reform on the argument that the current set up of the Autonomous Communities has nothing further to offer. Yet it is abundantly clear that they make these claims in a superficial way, being manifestly unable to justify their criticisms by putting forward alternatives.

Can the Constitution be read in a way that allows further development of the Autonomous Communities? It certainly can be, whether desirable or not. Several examples support this assumption. Let us remember the number of transfers of powers that were presented as being impossible before they were agreed and that finally went through with everyone's assent, and the deals made with Autonomous governments which were criticised by the opposition parties and then praised by the same parties once they came to power.[4] Not to mention the avenue opened up by Article 150.2 of the Constitution,[5] which has scarcely been used but which has had almost unanimous support in the Lower House in its application. The powers enjoyed by the Autonomous Communities can be increased both through open-minded interpretation of the Constitution itself and through application of the various routes it provides without any amendments being needed.

But can the demands now being made be dealt with within the framework of the Constitution? This is the problem. To find an answer, the demands must be clearly and accurately stated. Such a complicated question cannot be addressed unless it is posed in a specific and unequivocal way. The scope for action is very wide. Some of the recent demands are much more likely to be accepted now than a few years ago. The momentum gained in Autonomous Community-building now means that to have efficient self-government, the transfer of the specific allowable competencies of Article 148 should be complemented by new competencies that were initially retained by central government in Article 149. Lawmakers can use the various possible readings to opt for new interpretations of the Constitution that expand the boundaries for the transfer of powers to the Autonomous Communities, especially as regards the area of basic law.[6] And in the light of developments so far, it is not out of the question that the Constitutional Tribunal itself might reconsider some of its jurisprudence which now seems out of line with social changes.

A good example that the room for manoeuvre is considerable can be found in a new interpretation that emerged by consensus and allows conscription to be replaced by a professional army. Despite Article 30.2 providing for obligatory military service, this new consensus among all the political parties holds that it could be replaced by voluntary, professional forces. It goes without saying that any efforts to meet the new demands for autonomy are of lesser consequence than this one.

Differentials among the Autonomous Communities

I repeat, the margins for action are very wide, though my interpretation has its critics who claim that it will never solve the problem of differentials in powers demanded by some of the historic Communities as against generalised autonomy.[7] They claim that generalised autonomy leads to equalisation and that this is incompatible with the reality of plural nationalities within one state. This is the crux of the problem and should be examined in some detail.

Firstly, has the spread of autonomy to all regions of Spain put a stop to developing self-government in the historic Communities? Some say the whole problem stems from the constitutional decision to allow any region to accede to autonomy if it wishes. I do not share this view. On the contrary, over twenty years later, I believe that having self-government throughout Spain has smoothed the path to understanding our cultural pluralism. Of course, in theory, universal (nationwide) self-government does grant the Autonomous Communities the same level of *maximum* powers, but it has been rather different in reality. From the outset, the processes of implementation progressed at different speeds and the results have been divergent. Some Autonomous Communities have achieved transfers of powers that go beyond the maximum levels granted to the others. In any case, the 'differential facts' or distinctive features which define separate sub-national identities have led to powers being granted in the area of language, culture or law which the other Autonomous Communities cannot and should not claim.

For these reasons it is not true to say that universal autonomy has prevented Catalonia, for example, from having greater levels of self-government. True, on more than one occasion, certain transfers of powers have been delayed or even refused because of the fear of what this could mean for the state administration. But such behaviour should not be attributed to constitutional provisions, but rather to the biased and partisan fashion in which they have been interpreted. In general I would argue that none of the problems arising from the demands made for faster self-government have anything to do with the design of the Constitution.

Spain's Plurinational Composition

Another question is what does the Constitution mean when it mentions nationalities and regions and how does that fit into the debate? According to the text, Spain is made up of 'nationalities' and 'regions' – a phrase that shows that different realities are recognised. The Constitution does not say which is one or the other; neither does it define why the difference exists nor what consequences can be drawn from it. It simply recognises that they both exist and are different from each other. In fact we, the drafters, wanted to establish a dual recognition – whether this now seems like a good idea or not. On the one hand, Catalonia and the Basque Country, and to a lesser extent Galicia (as it was believed at the time), historically had their own distinct identity which granted them certain rights to effective self-government. For these historic nationalities, autonomy was not the result of any principle of subsidiarity[8] or any gesture of modernity. It was simply a long-standing demand which democracy had to meet.

There was nothing to stop nationalities and regions sharing a common form of state, but for the former the urgency of achieving self-government was mixed with the need for a more pluralistic state in which their own individual identities could reach an easy and respectful accommodation, something which had been denied them until then. While the State of Autonomous Communities is a reality which I believe to be irreversible, I admit there is still a problem with finding an answer to Spain's plurinational reality. Indeed very little progress has been made in this area.

It is an issue of identity, and of what defines the identity of the 'nationalities' within the nation-state of Spain. Are they exclusively a cultural phenomenon? Certainly they

83

are a fundamental cultural, linguistic and historic reality which has shaped their institutions and laws; but they are something more. They have, as the French historian Pierre Vilar says, a 'will to exist' or, to put it in my own words, *the nationalities have a different way of experiencing and understanding their right to self-government*; they are the fruit of a greater collective ambition.

For this reason, the views of those who claim to solve this problem only from the cultural perspective will not prevail – there is something more to it. Cultural or linguistic differences can be clearly expressed in terms of 'powers' (however controversial these may be) but the 'something extra' is more difficult to understand. The dividing lines are quite subtle and require a particular sensitivity for them to be fully grasped. When this is lacking, it all seems to fade away, yet seen through this prism, it all seems more comprehensible; without it, understanding seems to crumble.

How can this question be solved in practice? There is no need to amend the 1978 Constitution to meet the challenge. Proponents of 'asymmetric federalism' believe the Constitution, in practice, permits an asymmetric treatment of any matter that each identity claims as its own, leaving a common framework for the remainder. The result would not necessarily be homogenous, as the characteristic features and ambitions of each Community would be spelled out in different ways within the framework of the Constitution.

Even if an asymmetric treatment resolves the differences, there is still no answer to the issue of the 'something more' mentioned above, which needs definition. The greater vocation for self-government which is felt by some historic nationalities can be understood as a desire for a type of autonomy that is *qualitatively* different. While it may at first appear contradictory, increased levels of self-government can often be accompanied by additional needs, different from those of the Communities with less powers. So, logically, the lack of an effective system to finance the Autonomies is perceived *more* in the Communities with greater levels of self-government. Catalonia's tax-raising privileges have been used in all sorts of ways to incite resentment on the grounds of inequity, when in fact, all parties *could* accept that, the current financing system being inadequate, the Communities with greater responsibilities actually experience the inadequacy more painfully. Simply put, resources have not followed responsibilities. Yet no-one is offended by the Charter system that allows certain Spanish towns to have a different accounting regime from the rest. Economic exceptions could also be made on the basis of size.

An unbiased and equitable solution to this problem is urgently required and is fully compatible with the current constitutional framework. I am not suggesting that the Basque system of negotiated financial settlements (*concierto*)[9] should be expanded, but rather urging the adoption of a system, whatever system, which in practice has the same resource implications as those generated by the negotiated settlements in the Basque Country and Navarre. There is no constitutional rule to stop this. In fact this could be one function of the Constitution, expressly mentioned in the 1978 text, namely to guarantee a balanced distribution of state resources.

Senate Reform and Resource Distribution

For these reasons, the pending Senate reform, requiring constitutional amendment, should not be considered independently of the question of control of financial resources, so that, in time, a new form of the Senate can provide an appropriate instrument for such control to be effective. In this way the reform of the Senate would be a direct consequence of the new controls to regulate the Autonomous Communities' finances. As in federal states, the Spanish Senate is the arena for debate between the Autonomous Communities on such essential matters as the regional distribution of public funds. It would therefore be senseless to proceed to an urgent reform of the Senate without first having solved the problem of how to finance the Autonomous Communities – a problem which has nothing to do with constitutional reform per se.

Just as urgently as this financial control, the government needs to adopt policies and take steps which will symbolise its acceptance of the role of the Autonomous Communities as part of the Spanish State, since they represent the fundamental expression of the territorial organisation of the State. For despite this attribute also being granted to provinces and municipalities, the latter's purely administrative functions make the Autonomous Communities the territorial repositories of State power. And although the State has its own voice through its central institutions, without the Autonomous Communities, it would not be fully representative. This is felt particularly keenly in the historic Communities (Catalonia, Galicia and the Basque Country), who want to be consulted and to share in important State decisions. Their wishes are particularly important when it comes to having a say on matters affecting their powers, both domestically and on a European Union and international level. So, for instance, nationwide cultural policy should not be made without the agreement of the Autonomous Communities, since they are accepted as being 'nationalities' precisely because of their specific cultural and linguistic features.

To accept their difference would be in line with Article 9 of the Constitution requiring that public authorities remove the obstacles which prevent or constrain the fulfilment of freedom and equality of the individual. Accepting difference means respecting it and making its expression possible – all of which is provided for in the Constitution. But it would be quite something else to try to go beyond this.

State Unity

While the Constitution allows anything which is compatible with State unity, there is no possibility for independence for any part of Spain, nor for a confederation of autonomous parts (Article 141.1) – let us be clear about this. Not surprisingly, any hope for independence by any Community does not fall within the bounds of the Constitution. In fact, I would say this would not fundamentally be a constitutional problem but a political one. It is not even a question of the form of the State (federal or unitary) as it would affect the territorial and demographic identity of Spain and so would not be something which can be solved through an amendment of the Constitution, but rather, would require an alteration of the State itself. Still, even here a constitutional means to achieve this meta-constitutional goal could be found through dialogue and agreement on reforming the basic parts of the text. But it must be accepted that this question seems at odds with the constitutional will of any democratic country: secession is not a constitutional problem, it is a political challenge and can only be solved politically.

To return to the question of reform, leaving aside the matter of the Senate, there is *no* issue that justifies amending the text. For the effective recognition of Spain's plurinational reality, the Constitution contains sufficient mechanisms. The hopes expressed by the majority nationalist parties (Catalan Convergence and Union, Basque Nationalist Party) for recognition of the State's plurinational make-up can also be met without any need for reform. Contrary to appearances, the problems concerning the development of the Autonomous Communities do not originate in the inability of the constitutional text to provide an outlet, but rather in a political debate outside the confines of the Constitution. *In the final analysis, the Constitution is not the problem but rather the pretext for a more complex debate*, in which certain voices want reform more as a symbol of political victory than as an actual way to solve particular shortcomings.

Completing the Constitutional Order

Let us now consider the other matters which suggest the need to complement or complete our constitutional order in the light of recent political experience. It is not simply a question of *reforming* but also of *rethinking* some of the big questions that have raised their head at the end of the century in all Western democratic systems, but which the Spanish Constitution had neither the time nor the desire to consider in 1977–8.

I refer, for example, to the media deserving a mention in the Constitution. We are living in a media world (it's only real if we've seen it on TV, the medium is the message, and all that). The media's great ability to influence public opinion means that individual freedom can be compromised or at least subtly affected. This is not to downplay the important role that the new electronic media can have in strengthening democratic accountability and citizen participation. But there is no denying that they can shape the will of the people.

The issue is far wider than the rather petty, biased quarrels that have recently taken place over the regulation or otherwise of media groups by public institutions. Rather than discussing limit-setting, we should be recognising that there is a new scenario – the media society – to be added to the traditional division and balance of powers. It should greatly influence the classic framework for understanding where power lies. How to approach all this is outside the scope of my article, but when it comes to compiling a list of the points that a hypothetical constitutional reform should deal with in the future, I believe that the invasion of media power on a democratic system should clearly be included.

It is not unrelated to the question of the judiciary. How can the independence of the courts be guaranteed? What functions should the General Council of the Judiciary have?[10] How are the controllers supervised and by whom? All these are highly topical questions and there seem to be no precise answers. We should probably accept that constitutional regulation of the judiciary could be improved in the light of events that are known widely[11], but it is also true that many political errors were made in parliament and by government while developing the regulatory framework.

Here too, new procedures could be adopted to solve some of the more pressing problems without any need to amend the Constitution. The powers of the State Prosecutor's Office (*Ministerio Fiscal*), for example, could be defined more precisely to avoid the permanent confrontation between the legally enshrined principle of administrative hierarchy and the principle of autonomy demanded by individual prosecutors. It would be sufficient to amend existing parliamentary Acts, but even doing this would require a calmer political climate.

Another matter that is often cited as requiring amendment is the way in which the Constitution regulates the electoral system (e.g. Articles 68 and 69). The danger is that those who favour reforming it will not be able to agree and a debate would be kindled that would disturb one of the most peaceful elements of our political life. We have lived with this system since the first elections of 15 June 1977, and all its minor legislative amendments have been approved by very large majorities. Any future amendment should above all ensure that this consensus is maintained. It would be a terrible shame if a system that has already become part of our heritage should hencefoth become a battleground.

Conclusion

These thoughts are the result of my highly positive assessment of the role of our 1978 Constitution in promoting co-existence in democracy and freedom for everyone. It is not a paternalistic defence – it cannot be, because we were all party to the Constitution, it was not handed down from above – but rather the observations of a citizen who wishes to continue living in the system of freedom we have enjoyed for over twenty years.

Fortunately, we created a Constitution that can be widely and openly interpreted, which is adaptable to new circumstances and does not need to be recast. In the controversial matter of Autonomous Community development, the Constitution has allowed a spectacular change towards the decentralisation of political power and has established firmer foundations on which democratically to discuss where we go from here. In a way, recent political debates are proof of this: violence has had to give way to dialogue and claims are expressed within a framework of respect for the Constitution, even when reform is sought. This has even included respect for those who criticise it. As said earlier, we do not need to canonise the Constitution: reforming it would not be, nor should be, traumatic; it would simply be activating a constitutional procedure (Title X).

May neither discussion nor controversy obscure the central fact that we have enjoyed an exceptional twenty years and more of political normality, thanks to the spirit of consensus that gave birth to the 1978 Constitution.

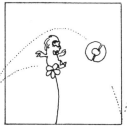

Los contenciosos entre la Generalidad y Madrid, en vías de solución (19 de diciembre de 1980)
Pujol restablece sus buenas relaciones con el Gobierno

Dispute between Catalonia and Madrid soon to be resolved
Pujol re-establishes good relations with government

Peridis's prophetic caricature of Jordi Pujol from 1980, already propping up a government (Suárez's), free-riding on both the UCD wheel and the PSOE rose and getting his way by playing one off against the other ('that convinced him'). It illustrated a headline that was to repeat itself many a time over the next 20 years.

Notes

1   The Senate is presently a hybrid chamber with directly elected Senators as well as designated ones from the Autonomous Communities (See Article 69.5). It is not, therefore, fully a chamber of territorial representation like the German Bundesrat.
2   Adversarial politics in the British context.
3   ETA announced the suspension of its 18-month truce in November 1999.
4   A reference to the blessing given by the Partido Popular to tax-raising powers for Catalonia.
5   In which the State can transfer or delegate to Autonomous Communities faculties relating to matters in the purview of the State, by means of a law which will also provide the relevant transfer of financial resources.
6   Which the State mostly retains for itself, in the Constitution.
7   Some argue for maintaining the original differential (greater powers) between historic and late-comer autonomies.
8   The principle derived from German federalism that decisions should be taken at the lowest tier of government possible.
9   The *conciertos* are the special agreements granting the Basque government a right to levy nearly all taxes in that autonomous community (See Newton, M., *op.cit.* p.130).
10 The highest governing body of the judiciary which has authority over appointments, training and promotion and disciplinary matters.
11 Both the PSOE and the PP governments altered the method of election of the Council's members.

Translation by Kathryn Phillips-Miles and Monica Threlfall.
All footnotes by the editor.